THE ULTIMATE GUIDE TO BUSINESS PROFESSIONALISM

Business Coordination, Your Greatest Asset.

TONY B. SCOTT

This book is a work of nonfiction. The names, characters, places, and incidents are products of the author's imagination or are used fictitiously. Any resemblance to actual events, locales, or persons, living or dead, is entirely coincidental.

Overview of Professionalism in the Business World

An overview of professionalism in the business world encompasses several key dimensions that collectively define how individuals present themselves, interact with others, and fulfill their roles within a professional setting. Professionalism is not just about one's appearance or punctuality, though these elements are important; it's more broadly about the attitude, behavior, ethics, and standards one upholds in a business environment. Understanding and embodying professionalism helps individuals to advance their careers, fosters a positive workplace culture, and contributes to the success of their organization.

Key Components of Professionalism
1. Communication Skills: Effective communication is crucial. This includes not just verbal communication but also non-verbal cues and written correspondence. Professionals must be able to clearly convey ideas, listen actively, and respond appropriately in various situations. Email etiquette, presentation skills, and the ability to negotiate or persuade are also part of this domain.

2. Ethical Behavior: This entails adhering to the moral principles and standards of conduct expected in the business world, including honesty, integrity, fairness, and respect for others.

Professionals must ensure that their actions and decisions are not just legally compliant but also ethically sound.

3. Reliability and Accountability: A hallmark of professionalism is being dependable and taking responsibility for one's actions. This means meeting deadlines, keeping promises, and being prepared. When mistakes happen, professionals own up to them and work towards rectifying the situation rather than evading responsibility.

4. Competence: Continual learning and skill development are vital. Professionals strive to maintain a high level of competency in their field, staying updated with the latest knowledge, trends, and technologies that affect their profession. This commitment to excellence ensures that they can perform their duties effectively and contribute value.

5.   Respectful   Behavior: Professionalism involves treating colleagues, clients, and all other stakeholders with respect and courtesy. This includes being mindful of cultural differences, maintaining confidentiality where required, and fostering an inclusive environment that values diversity.

6. Appearance and Demeanor: While less emphasized than other aspects, the way a person dresses and conducts themselves still plays a role in professional settings. Adhering to dress codes, exhibiting good manners, and maintaining a composed demeanor contribute to a positive and professional image.

Impact of Professionalism

Professionalism influences not just individual success but also the operational effectiveness of organizations. It builds trust among team members, enhances the reputation of the company, and can lead to higher customer satisfaction. In an increasingly global and competitive market, professionalism can differentiate individuals and companies, driving growth and fostering sustainable relationships.

Challenges and Considerations

In the dynamic landscape of the modern business world, the concept of professionalism evolves. The rise of remote work, the integration of new technologies, and changing societal norms all impact what is considered professional behavior. Therefore, individuals and organizations must be adaptable, continually reassessing and updating their standards of professionalism to stay relevant and effective.

In conclusion, professionalism is a multifaceted concept that is integral to the fabric of the business world. It encompasses a wide range of behaviors and attitudes that, when practiced diligently, can enhance both individual careers and the broader organizational culture. As the business environment continues to evolve, so will the expectations and manifestations of professionalism, making it an ongoing journey of growth and adaptation for professionals worldwide.

Chapter 1: Introduction to Business Professionalism

Introduction to Business Professionalism
In the competitive and evolving landscape of the business world, professionalism stands out as a cornerstone that can significantly impact the trajectory of an individual's career and the overall success of an organization. At its core, business professionalism is a blend of qualities, behaviors, and standards that are widely recognized and respected within a workplace or industry. It serves as a guiding framework that shapes how individuals conduct themselves in a

business context, encompassing everything from interpersonal interactions to the ethical considerations guiding decision-making processes.

Defining Business Professionalism

Professionalism in a business context can be multi-dimensional, comprising various elements that contribute to a positive and productive work environment. It is not merely about adhering to a specific dress code or following a set of rigid rules; rather, it embodies a broader ethos that influences actions, communication, and attitudes. Key components include:

Ethical Practice: Upholding integrity, honesty, and accountability in all business dealings to foster trust and respect among colleagues, clients, and stakeholders.

Communication Skills: Effective and clear communication, both verbal and written, ensuring respectful and constructive interactions.

Reliability: Consistency in performance and dependability in meeting commitments and responsibilities.

Competence: Maintaining a high level of knowledge and skill in your area of expertise, and committing to continuous learning and improvement.

Respect: Displaying courteous behavior towards everyone in the professional sphere, acknowledging diverse perspectives, and valuing contributions from all team members.

Appropriate Appearance: Dressing and presenting oneself in a manner that reflects well on the individual and the organization, suitable to the context and culture of the workplace.

Importance of Professionalism

Professionalism is pivotal for several reasons. First, it creates a positive first impression, which can be crucial in business relationships. Second, it establishes a foundation of trust and reliability that is essential for effective teamwork and collaboration. Professional behavior also contributes to a conducive work environment, enhancing productivity and satisfaction among employees. Furthermore, it reinforces the reputation of an organization, attracting talent and clients who value a professional culture.

Cultivating Professionalism.

Developing professionalism is an ongoing process that involves self-awareness, observation, and feedback.

Individuals can cultivate professionalism by:

Setting High Standards: Aim for excellence in all aspects of your work and behavior.

Seeking Feedback: Regular feedback from peers, supervisors, and mentors can provide valuable insights into areas for improvement.

Observing Role Models: Learning from the example of respected professionals in your field can offer guidance on how to navigate various situations with professionalism.

Continuous Learning: Staying informed about your industry, improving your skills, and expanding your knowledge base are essential for maintaining competence and relevance.

Adapting to Change: The business world is constantly evolving, and so are the definitions and expectations around professionalism. Flexibility and adaptability are crucial in meeting these changing standards.

Challenges to Professionalism

While the concept of professionalism seems straightforward, real-world application can present challenges. Navigating cultural differences, adapting to new modes of communication (e.g., virtual meetings and remote work), and maintaining ethical standards in complex situations are just a few of the dilemmas that professionals might encounter. Overcoming these challenges requires a commitment to the core principles of professionalism, coupled with the ability to adapt to the nuances of each unique context.

Conclusion

In essence, business professionalism encapsulates the principles and behaviors that foster respect, competence, and ethical practices within the workplace. It serves not only as a benchmark for individual conduct but also as a building block for organizational culture. By embracing and promoting professionalism, businesses can create environments that nurture success, innovation, and mutual respect – ultimately contributing to their long-term growth and sustainability in a competitive global landscape.

Definition of Professionalism

Definition of Professionalism

Professionalism is a multifaceted concept that encapsulates the attitudes, behaviors, and standards that are expected of individuals within a professional setting. It is the framework upon which individuals build their work ethic, interact with others, and present themselves in their careers. Professionalism goes beyond the mere acquisition of skills and knowledge; it involves a commitment to ethical practices, effective communication, and continuous improvement in service to oneself, one's profession, and society at large.

Core Elements of Professionalism

Understanding professionalism requires dissecting its core components, which include but are not limited to:

1. **Competence**: At the heart of professionalism lies competence—possession of the required skills and knowledge to perform one's job efficiently. This includes staying up to date with advancements in one's field and continuously seeking personal and professional development.

2. **Ethical Behavior**: Professionalism is deeply rooted in ethics. It demands adherence to the moral principles and standards that govern a profession, including integrity, accountability, and the prioritization of the client's or employer's interests over personal gain.

3. **Reliability**: Professionals are expected to be dependable and trustworthy, consistently delivering quality work on time and meeting or exceeding expectations.

4. Respect: This entails treating all colleagues, clients, and stakeholders with dignity, politeness, and understanding, regardless of differences in opinion, background, or status. It also encompasses the ability to work collaboratively in a team, valuing the contributions of others.

5. Communication: Effective communication skills are essential. This not only includes clear and concise verbal and written communication but also active listening, the ability to give and receive feedback constructively, and the prowess to communicate complex information understandably.

6. Appearance: In many professions, adhering to a certain standard of dress and personal appearance is a reflection of respect for the job, the clientele, and oneself. While what is considered appropriate can vary widely across different fields, presenting oneself in a clean, orderly, and professionally acceptable manner is a universal aspect of professionalism.

The Importance of Professionalism:
Professionalism is critical for several reasons:
Trust Building: It forms the foundation of trust between professionals and their clients, colleagues, and the broader community.

Career Advancement: Exhibiting professionalism can lead to career growth opportunities, as it is often a key factor in evaluations for promotions and recognitions.

Workplace Environment: A culture of professionalism within an organization promotes a positive, respectful, and productive workplace environment.

Reputation: Both individuals and organizations benefit from the reputation of professionalism, which can attract clients, partners, and talented employees.

Ethical Standards: Upholding professionalism ensures that ethical standards are maintained, which is crucial in fields that directly impact the well-being of others.

Challenges to Professionalism

In the modern world, professionalism faces challenges from rapidly evolving work environments, such as the rise of remote work, which has changed traditional perceptions of professionalism in terms of dress codes and working hours. Moreover, the increasing reliance on digital communication tools requires professionals to adapt their communication skills to maintain professionalism online.

Conclusion

Professionalism is an integral part of the fabric that makes up the work environment and professional interactions. It is not static but evolves with changing societal norms, technological advancements, and shifts in the professional landscape. Regardless of these changes, the foundational elements of professionalism remain constant, serving as a guiding light for individuals striving to embody the highest standards of their profession. Understanding and adhering to these principles of professionalism not only enhances individual careers but also contributes significantly to the integrity and effectiveness of the professional community as a whole.

The Importance of Professionalism in Business

The Importance of Professionalism in Business.

In the competitive and dynamic environment of modern business, professionalism acts as a cornerstone of success. It is a comprehensive concept that transcends industry boundaries, encompassing a set of behaviors, attitudes, and practices essential for individuals and organizations aiming to maintain excellence, foster positive relationships, and achieve long-term goals. The importance of professionalism in business cannot be overstated; it is integral to building trust, enhancing company reputation, facilitating communication, and driving personal and organizational growth.

Building Trust and Credibility

At the foundation of every successful business relationship lies trust. Professionalism, through its emphasis on ethical behavior, reliability, and competence, fosters a sense of dependability among customers, clients, and colleagues. When individuals act with integrity and accountability, they build a reputation of trustworthiness that, in turn, attracts and retains clients and customers. This credibility is crucial not only for individual success but also for the organization's longevity and reputation in the market.

Enhancing Corporate Image and Reputation.

Professionalism directly influences the public image and reputation of a business. Organizations known for maintaining high standards of professionalism are more likely to be viewed positively by customers, investors, and the public. This encompasses everything from the way employees interact with stakeholders to how the company responds to challenges and errors. A professional corporate image bolsters confidence in the brand, leading to increased customer loyalty and a stronger competitive edge.

Facilitating Effective Communication

Effective communication is a vital element of professionalism that impacts nearly every aspect of business operations. Professional communication, characterized by clarity, respect, and appropriateness, ensures that messages are conveyed and received as intended, reducing misunderstandings and conflicts. It also enhances decision-making processes and collaboration among teams, contributing to smoother project management and workflow.

Fostering a Positive Workplace Culture. Professionalism contributes significantly to creating and maintaining a positive, respectful workplace culture. When employees exhibit professional behavior—treating each other with respect, taking responsibility for their actions, and valuing diversity and inclusion—they create an environment where people feel valued and supported. This positive atmosphere not only improves employee satisfaction and engagement but also attracts top talent, as prospective employees are drawn to workplaces that demonstrate respect and fairness.

Driving Growth and Adaptability

In a rapidly changing business environment, professionalism embodies the adaptability and continuous learning required for sustained growth. By committing to professional development, individuals and organizations can stay ahead of industry trends, technological advancements, and evolving customer needs. This openness to growth and learning fosters innovation and ensures that businesses remain competitive and relevant.

Ensuring Ethical Standards

Professionalism serves as a safeguard for ethical standards in business practices. It demands adherence to moral principles, guiding individuals and organizations to make decisions that are not only legally compliant but also ethically sound. In industries where the potential for ethical dilemmas is high, professionalism provides a framework for navigating complex situations, ensuring that actions taken are in the best interest of all stakeholders.

Mitigating Conflicts and Building Team Cohesion

Professional behavior plays a crucial role in conflict resolution and team cohesion. By promoting respectful communication, empathy, and a focus on solutions, professionalism helps mitigate conflicts before they escalate into more significant issues. Additionally, a professional approach to collaboration and problem-solving encourages team unity and cooperation, essential elements for achieving common goals and objectives.

Conclusion

The importance of professionalism in business extends far beyond the surface level of attire or etiquette; it is about creating a foundation of trust, respect, and ethical behavior that permeates every aspect of an organization's operations. It influences how businesses are perceived by the outside world, how they communicate internally and externally, and how they navigate the challenges and opportunities of the modern business landscape. Ultimately, professionalism is a key driver of success, fostering environments where businesses and individuals can thrive and achieve their fullest potential.

Historical Context and Evolution of Business Professionalism

Historical Context and Evolution of Business Professionalism.

The concept of professionalism in the business world has evolved significantly over centuries, deeply influenced by social, economic, and technological changes. This evolution reflects broader shifts in work culture, economic structures, and societal values, with each phase introducing new norms and expectations for individuals in the workplace.

Pre-Industrial Times.

The roots of professionalism can be traced back to the guilds of medieval Europe, where craftsmen organized themselves into associations based on trade or skill. These guilds established standards for quality, defined ethical practices, and set entry requirements for new practitioners. Although not business professionalism in today's sense, these early practices laid the groundwork by emphasizing skill, ethics, and community standards.

Industrial Revolution to the 20th Century
The Industrial Revolution brought about profound changes, transitioning economies from agrarian to industrial bases and fundamentally altering the nature of work. This period saw the rise of factories and the separation of home from workplace, which brought about new organizational structures and management practices. Professionalism during this era became closely associated with the emerging managerial class, introducing concepts like punctuality,

regularity, and a more formalized work ethic.

In the late 19th and early 20th centuries, the growth of corporations and the expansion of consumer markets led to the development of modern business practices. This period saw the professionalization of various fields, including accounting, marketing, and human resources, which became recognized as essential disciplines within the business environment. Professional associations and institutes were established to standardize practices, certify professionals, and promote ethical standards.

Post-World War II Era

The post-WWII era marked a significant expansion in the concept of professionalism. The economic boom, technological advancements, and the growth of corporate America contributed to a burgeoning middle class and an expanded role for professionals. Business professionalism during this time emphasized corporate loyalty, a strong work ethic, and conformity to company culture, reflecting the societal values of stability and progress.

Late 20th Century to the Digital Age

The late 20th century introduced significant shifts with the advent of the information technology revolution and globalization. These changes impacted the very nature of work, leading to more knowledge-based professions and a greater focus on individual autonomy, flexibility, and work-life balance. Professionalism began to incorporate the ability to adapt to rapid technological changes, cultural sensitivity in an increasingly global marketplace, and a stronger emphasis on ethical responsibility and social impact.

The digital age further accelerated these trends, with the widespread adoption of the internet and digital technologies transforming how businesses operate and compete. Professionalism now encompasses digital literacy, virtual communication skills, and an ability to work effectively in decentralized and often remote teams. The rise of the gig economy and the increasing importance of personal branding on social media platforms have also influenced contemporary understandings of professionalism, underscoring the blend of personal and professional identities.

Conclusion

The evolution of business professionalism is a reflection of broader historical shifts in work, society, and technology. From the guilds of the medieval period to the digital workplaces of today, the concept of professionalism has expanded to include a wide array of skills, values, and behaviors. Looking forward, it is clear that professionalism will continue to evolve in response to new technological advancements, changing societal expectations, and the ongoing reconfiguration of the global economy. What remains constant, however, is the core emphasis on ethics, competence, and commitment to excellence that defines professionalism across eras.

Chapter 2: The Pillars of Professionalism

The Pillars of Professionalism.

Professionalism is a multifaceted principle that serves as the bedrock of workplace conduct and ethics. It encompasses a broad spectrum of behaviors, attitudes, and practices essential for individuals to effectively navigate and contribute to their professional environment. While professionalism can manifest differently across industries and organizational cultures, there are foundational pillars that universally underpin this concept. Understanding these pillars is crucial for anyone looking to embody professionalism in their career.

1. Competence

One of the most critical pillars of professionalism is competence, which refers to possessing the necessary skills, knowledge, and expertise to perform one's job effectively. This involves not only the initial acquisition of relevant qualifications but also a commitment to ongoing learning and development. Professionals strive to stay abreast of industry trends, technological advancements, and best practices to ensure their contributions are valuable and up to date.

2. Integrity.

Integrity encompasses honesty, ethical behavior, and a strong moral principle in every action and decision. Professionals with integrity are trustworthy, reliable, and straightforward in their dealings, fostering an environment of transparency and trust. This pillar is crucial in building and maintaining solid relationships with clients, colleagues, and stakeholders, ensuring that interactions are conducted respectfully and ethically.

3. Accountability

Accountability is the willingness to take responsibility for one's actions and their outcomes, whether positive or negative. It involves acknowledging mistakes, learning from them, and taking steps to correct them. Professionals who embody accountability demonstrate a commitment to high standards and continuous improvement, thereby fostering respect and credibility within their professional circle.

4. Respect.

Professionalism requires showing respect to everyone, regardless of their position, background, or opinions. This includes polite and considerate communication, valuing other people's time and contributions, and maintaining a positive, empathetic demeanor. A respectful professional environment encourages collaboration, inclusion, and diversity, making it a fundamental pillar of professionalism.

5. Ethical Decision-making.

Professionals often face decisions that test their values and ethical standards. Ethical decision-making involves choosing actions that are not only legally compliant but also morally sound and aligned with the values of the profession and organization. This pillar is particularly significant in professions where the stakes are high, and decisions can significantly impact individuals, communities, and the environment.

6. Reliability

Being reliable means consistently meeting expectations, fulfilling commitments, and delivering high-quality work. Reliability builds confidence among team members, clients, and superiors, establishing a reputation for dependability. This pillar is essential for the smooth operation of professional engagements and for forging long-term, trust-based relationships.

7. Communication

Effective communication skills, both verbal and written, are indispensable in maintaining professionalism. Clear, concise, and respectful communication ensures that ideas and information are accurately conveyed, misunderstandings are minimized, and collaborative efforts are streamlined. Additionally, being an active listener is equally important, as it demonstrates respect and understanding toward others' viewpoints.

8. Appearance and Demeanor

Although often considered less critical than other pillars, appearance and demeanor play a significant role in professionalism. Dressing appropriately for one's role and maintaining a positive, composed demeanor contribute to making a good impression, embodying the organization's values, and setting a standard for the workplace environment.

Conclusion

The pillars of professionalism create a framework for ethical, effective, and respectful interaction within the professional sphere. Embracing these principles is essential for anyone looking to advance their career and contribute positively to their organization and industry. Moreover, as the business world continues to evolve with technological advancements and socio-economic changes, these pillars offer a stable foundation upon which professionals can adapt and thrive in new and challenging contexts.

- Integrity and Ethics

Integrity and Ethics: The Cornerstones of Professional Conduct.

Integrity and ethics are fundamental principles that form the cornerstone of professional behavior in any field or industry. While integrity relates to personal honesty and moral uprightness, ethics refer to a set of standards that guide behavior within a specific context, such as a profession or organization. Together, integrity and ethics create a framework for individuals to make principled decisions, uphold moral values, and maintain trust and credibility in their professional interactions.

Integrity: The Core of Personal Character. Honesty, ethics, and a firm sense of moral principles are characteristics of integrity. It is a personal attribute that underpins an individual's actions and decisions, reflecting a consistency between what is said and what is done. Professionals with integrity demonstrate reliability, truthfulness, and transparency in all their interactions, building trust with colleagues, clients, and stakeholders.

Key Aspects of Integrity:

1. **Honesty**: Being truthful and forthright in communication, actions, and intentions.

2. **Consistency**: Aligning actions with values and maintaining integrity across different situations.

3. **Accountability**: Taking responsibility for one's actions and their outcomes, whether positive or negative.

4. **Trustworthiness**: Inspiring confidence and reliance through reliability, credibility, and ethical behavior.

5. **Transparency**: Operating with openness, clarity, and disclosure in dealings and decision-making processes.

Ethics: Guiding Principles for Professional Conduct.

Ethics are a set of moral principles that govern behavior and decision-making within a particular context. Professional ethics outline the standards and values that individuals in a profession should adhere to, ensuring integrity, fairness, and respect in their interactions. Ethical behavior goes beyond legal compliance, requiring individuals to consider the broader impact of their actions on stakeholders and society.

Key Aspects of Ethics:

1. **Respect:** Treating others with dignity, fairness, and consideration, regardless of differences.

2. **Justice:** Upholding fairness, equity, and impartiality in decision-making and actions.

3. **Beneficence:** Acting in ways that benefit others and contribute to their well-being.

4. **Non-maleficence:** Avoiding harm or injury to others and preventing negative repercussions.

5. Confidentiality: Safeguarding sensitive information and respecting individuals' privacy and trust.

Importance of Integrity and Ethics in Professional Environments:

Integrity and ethics serve as crucial pillars of professional conduct, underpinning trust, accountability, and credibility within organizations and industries. Upholding these principles contributes to a positive workplace culture, fosters strong relationships with clients and partners, and enhances the reputation of individuals and organizations in the long term.

Benefits of Upholding Integrity and Ethics:

1. Trust and Credibility: Building trust among colleagues, clients, and stakeholders through consistent, ethical behavior.

2. **Professional Reputation**: Enhancing personal and organizational reputation by demonstrating integrity and ethical decision-making.

3. **Conflict Resolution**: Facilitating fair and just resolutions in conflicts and ethical dilemmas through principled actions.

4. **Employee Morale**: Promoting a positive work environment and high employee morale by upholding ethical standards.

5. **Compliance and Risk Management**: Mitigating legal and ethical risks by adhering to ethical guidelines and regulatory requirements.

Conclusion

Integrity and ethics stand at the heart of professional conduct, guiding individuals to make principled decisions, maintain moral standards, and uphold the trust and respect of others. By embodying integrity and adhering to ethical principles, professionals not only enhance their own credibility and reputation but also contribute to a culture of ethics and integrity within their organizations and industries. As ethical considerations continue to play a prominent role in modern workplaces and society at large, embracing integrity and ethics remains essential for fostering responsible, trustworthy, and sustainable professional relationships and practices.

Accountability and Responsibility

Accountability and Responsibility in Professional Environments:

Accountability and responsibility are key principles that govern professional conduct, guiding individuals to take ownership of their actions, fulfill their duties, and adhere to ethical standards. While accountability involves answerability for outcomes and decisions, responsibility encompasses the obligations and duties one has towards their role, organization, and stakeholders. Together, these principles create a framework for transparent, reliable, and ethical behavior in professional environments.

Accountability: The Obligation to Answer for Actions.

Accountability is the willingness to accept responsibility for one's actions, decisions, and outcomes. It involves being answerable for the impact of one's conduct on oneself, colleagues, clients, and the organization as a whole. Professionals who embrace accountability take ownership of their work, admit mistakes, and work towards solutions to rectify errors or shortcomings.

Key Aspects of Accountability:

1. **Transparency:** Communicating openly and honestly about actions and decisions.

2. **Ownership:** Taking responsibility for the results of one's actions and performance.

3.   **Follow-through**: Fulfilling commitments and meeting expectations within agreed-upon timelines.

4. **Learning Orientation**: Viewing mistakes as opportunities for growth and improvement.

5. **Feedback Receptivity**: Accepting feedback and incorporating it into future actions and behaviors.

Responsibility: The Obligation to Fulfill Duties and Obligations.

Responsibility refers to the set of obligations, roles, and duties that individuals have within their professional sphere. It involves meeting expectations, delivering on commitments, and upholding ethical standards in line with one's role and the organization's mission and values. Professionals who embrace responsibility proactively engage in tasks, demonstrate reliability, and work towards achieving shared goals.

Key Aspects of Responsibility:

1. **Role Clarity**: Understanding one's position, expectations, and contributions within the organization.

2. **Task Completion**: Executing duties and assignments to the best of one's ability and within specified parameters.

3. **Ethical Compliance**: Adhering to moral principles, values, and standards that govern professional conduct.

4. **Team Contribution**: Collaborating with colleagues, sharing knowledge, and supporting shared objectives.

5. **Organizational Alignment**: Ensuring actions are aligned with the goals and mission of the organization.

Importance of Accountability and Responsibility in Professional Environments:

Accountability and responsibility play crucial roles in fostering a positive work culture, enhancing trust, and driving individual and organizational effectiveness. By embracing these principles, professionals contribute to a climate of transparency, reliability, and integrity, which are essential for sustainable growth and success in the workplace.

Benefits of Upholding Accountability and Responsibility:

1. **Trust and Credibility**: Building trust among colleagues and stakeholders through consistent and reliable behavior.

2. **Problem Solving**: Facilitating effective conflict resolution and decision-making

by taking ownership and seeking solutions.

3. Organizational Efficiency: Enhancing workflow and productivity by ensuring tasks are completed timely and effectively.

4. Professional Development: Fostering personal growth and skill development through a learning-oriented approach to tasks and challenges.

5. Ethical Standards: Upholding ethical values and promoting a culture of integrity and responsibility within the organization.

Conclusion

Accountability and responsibility are foundational principles that guide professional behavior, promote ethical conduct, and enhance trust and credibility in the workplace. By embodying these principles, individuals contribute to a culture of transparency, reliability, and mutual respect, fostering collaboration, innovation, and long-term success within their organizations. As the demands of the modern workplace continue to evolve, embracing accountability and responsibility remains essential for individuals to navigate challenges, drive positive change, and uphold the principles of integrity and ethical conduct in their professional endeavors.

Diligence and Excellence

Diligence and Excellence in Professional Practice:

Diligence and excellence are two interrelated principles that underpin high performance and quality outcomes in professional practice. Diligence involves persistent effort, attention to detail, and a steadfast commitment to completing tasks thoroughly and effectively. Excellence, on the other hand, encompasses the ongoing pursuit of superior performance, the delivery of exceptional results, and the continuous refinement of one's skills and knowledge. Together, diligence and excellence create a framework for achieving high standards of work and professional success.

Diligence: The Commitment to Thoroughness and Persistence.

Diligence is the quality of being careful, persistent, and attentive in one's work. It involves giving close attention to detail, maintaining focus on tasks, and demonstrating a strong work ethic throughout the completion of assignments. Professionals who exhibit diligence go the extra mile to ensure that tasks are completed accurately, efficiently, and to the best of their ability.

Key Aspects of Diligence:

1. **Attention to Detail**: Thoroughly reviewing work, checking for errors, and ensuring accuracy.

2. **Persistence:** Maintaining focus and determination, even in the face of challenges or setbacks.

3. **Consistency:** Demonstrating reliability and dedication in performing tasks over time.

4. **Time Management:** Prioritizing tasks, setting realistic goals, and using time efficiently.

5. **Quality Focus:** Striving for excellence in every aspect of work and not settling for mediocrity.

Excellence: The Pursuit of Superior Performance and Continuous Improvement.

Excellence is the relentless pursuit of superior performance, the achievement of outstanding results, and the continuous quest for improvement and innovation. It involves setting high standards, pushing boundaries, and consistently delivering work that goes above and beyond what is expected. Professionals who embody excellence inspire others, drive success, and shape a culture of achievement and growth.

Key Aspects of Excellence:

1. **High Standards:** Setting and maintaining lofty benchmarks for performance and quality.

2. **Innovation:** Encouraging creativity, originality, and proactive problem-solving in all endeavors.

3. Continuous Learning: Seeking opportunities for growth, skill development, and knowledge enhancement.

4. Feedback Integration: Embracing feedback, both positive and constructive, to fuel personal and professional growth.

5. Leadership by Example: Inspiring others through actions and setting a standard of excellence for the team or organization.

Importance of Diligence and Excellence in Professional Environments:

Diligence and excellence are critical components of professional success, driving productivity, innovation, and long-term growth in organizations. By upholding these principles, professionals can deliver high-quality work, foster a culture of continuous improvement, and elevate their personal and organizational performance to new heights.

Benefits of Embodying Diligence and Excellence:

1. **Quality Results:** Achieving superior outcomes and delivering work of the highest caliber.

2. **Professional Reputation:** Building a reputation for reliability, competency, and superior performance.

3. **Career Advancement:** Opening opportunities for growth, promotion, and increased responsibility.

4. **Team Success:** Inspiring and motivating colleagues to strive for excellence and achieve collective goals.

5. **Innovation and Progress**: Fostering a culture of creativity, improvement, and forward-thinking within the organization.

Conclusion

Diligence and excellence are integral principles that drive success, innovation, and personal growth in professional environments. By embodying a strong work ethic, attention to detail, and a commitment to continuous improvement, individuals can elevate their performance, contribute to organizational success, and make a lasting impact in their field. As professionals navigate the challenges and opportunities of the modern workplace, embracing diligence and excellence remains essential for achieving high standards of work, fostering a culture of achievement, and realizing their full potential in their professional endeavors.

Chapter 3: Communication Skills for Professionals

Communication Skills for Professionals:

Effective communication skills are essential for professionals across all industries and roles. Communication forms the foundation of successful interactions, collaboration, and relationship-building in the workplace. Strong communication skills not only enhance productivity and efficiency but also contribute to a positive work environment, effective leadership, and career advancement. This comprehensive note explores the key aspects of communication skills crucial for professionals in today's dynamic and interconnected business landscape.

Verbal Communication:

Verbal communication involves the spoken word and plays a key role in conveying messages, ideas, and information in the workplace. Effective verbal communication encompasses clarity, conciseness, and active listening. Professionals who excel in verbal communication can articulate thoughts clearly, engage in productive discussions, and ensure mutual understanding with colleagues, clients, and stakeholders.

Written Communication:

Written communication is equally important in professional environments, especially in a digitally-driven world. Strong writing skills are essential for composing clear and professional emails, reports, proposals, and other written documents. Professionals proficient in written communication can convey complex information effectively, maintain professionalism in written correspondence, and ensure their messages are well-received and understood by recipients.

Nonverbal Communication:
Nonverbal communication, including body language, facial expressions, gestures, and tone of voice, can significantly impact interpersonal interactions in the workplace. Professionals should be mindful of their nonverbal cues to convey confidence, respect, and attentiveness. Awareness of nonverbal communication can help professionals build trust, establish rapport, and navigate sensitive situations effectively.

Listening Skills:

A vital element of good communication is active listening. Professionals who actively listen demonstrate empathy, understanding, and respect for the speaker. Actively listening to colleagues, clients, and team members fosters better relationships, reduces misunderstandings, and enables more productive collaborations. Developing strong listening skills is essential for building trust and promoting open communication in professional settings.

Emotional Intelligence:

Emotional intelligence plays a significant role in communication effectiveness. Professionals with high emotional intelligence can navigate challenging conversations, manage conflicts, and build strong relationships based on empathy and understanding. Emotional intelligence enables professionals to communicate with sensitivity, address colleagues' emotions and concerns, and foster a positive and supportive work environment.

Adaptability in Communication:

The modern workplace is diverse and dynamic, requiring professionals to adapt their communication style to different audiences, channels, and situations. Being adaptable in communication involves tailoring messages based on the preferences and needs of the recipient, adjusting communication approaches in response to feedback, and effectively communicating across various platforms and mediums. Adaptability in communication allows professionals to connect with others effectively and navigate diverse and evolving work environments.

Conflict Resolution and Feedback:
Effective communication skills are crucial in conflict resolution and providing constructive feedback. Professionals adept at conflict resolution can navigate disagreements, address issues collaboratively, and find mutually beneficial solutions. Providing constructive feedback requires clarity, empathy, and specificity to help colleagues grow, improve performance, and achieve their professional goals.

Conclusion

Strong communication skills are indispensable for professionals seeking to succeed and thrive in today's fast-paced and interconnected business world. By honing their verbal and written communication, mastering nonverbal cues, practicing active listening, developing emotional intelligence, and being adaptable in their communication approach, professionals can build strong relationships, foster collaboration, and achieve their professional objectives effectively. Continuous improvement in communication skills not only enhances individual effectiveness but also contributes to a positive work culture, successful teamwork, and overall organizational success in the ever-evolving landscape of the modern workplace.

Verbal Communication: Clarity and Tone

Verbal Communication: Clarity and Tone: Verbal communication is a fundamental aspect of professional interactions, encompassing the spoken word and vocal delivery in conveying messages, exchanging information, and building relationships. Achieving clarity and setting an appropriate tone are essential components of effective verbal communication in the workplace. Clarity ensures that messages are easily understandable and free from ambiguity, while tone influences how messages are received, conveying emotions, attitudes, and intentions. This comprehensive note delves into the significance of clarity and tone in verbal communication for professionals and explores strategies to enhance both aspects for successful interpersonal exchanges.

Clarity in Verbal Communication:

1. **Enunciation and Pronunciation**: Articulating words clearly and correctly to ensure they are understood by the listener.

2. **Avoiding Jargon and Acronyms**: Using language that is concise and accessible, avoiding industry-specific terms that may not be understood by all.

3. **Structuring Messages**: Organizing thoughts and ideas logically to deliver information in a coherent and organized manner.

4. **Simplifying Complex Information**: Breaking down complex concepts into

digestible chunks to enhance comprehension.

5. Summarizing and Confirming: Reiterating key points and asking for confirmation to ensure understanding on both ends.

Setting an Appropriate Tone in Verbal Communication:

1. Positive and Engaging Tone: Maintaining a friendly, upbeat demeanor to foster rapport and engagement in conversations.

2. Empathetic and Supportive Tone: Demonstrating understanding, empathy, and support when addressing sensitive or challenging topics.

3. Professional and Respectful Tone: Maintaining professionalism and respect in all interactions, regardless of the circumstances.

4. Confidence and Assertiveness: Speaking with confidence and assertiveness to convey authority and credibility in one's message.

5. Adapting Tone to Context: Tailoring tone based on the context, audience, and nature of the conversation to ensure appropriateness and effectiveness.

Strategies to Enhance Verbal Communication: Clarity and Tone:

1. Practice Active Listening: Paying attention to verbal cues and nonverbal signals to respond empathetically and adjust communication as needed.

2. Seek Feedback: Soliciting feedback from colleagues or mentors to improve clarity, tone, and overall effectiveness of verbal communication.

3. Use Visualization Techniques: Visualizing the intended message and desired tone before speaking to enhance clarity and emotional resonance.

4. Engage in Role-Play: Practicing different communication scenarios through role-play to experiment with tone and refine verbal delivery.

5. Utilize Pause and Reflect: Taking pauses during conversations to reflect on clarity, tone, and message alignment before continuing.

Importance of Verbal Communication: Clarity and Tone in Professional Environments:

Effective verbal communication, characterized by clarity and appropriate tone, is vital for fostering understanding, building relationships, and driving successful outcomes in professional settings. Clear and well-articulated messages enhance comprehension, reduce misunderstandings, and promote collaboration, while an appropriate tone conveys professionalism, respect, and emotional intelligence. By mastering clarity and tone in verbal communication, professionals can enhance their credibility, influence, and overall effectiveness in interpersonal interactions, ultimately contributing to a positive and productive work environment.

Conclusion

Verbal communication forms the basis of effective professional interactions, with clarity and tone being essential elements for successful communication outcomes. By prioritizing clarity to ensure messages are easily understood, and adopting appropriate tones to convey emotions, attitudes, and intentions effectively, professionals can enhance their communication skills and build strong relationships in the workplace. Through practice, feedback, and mindfulness, professionals can refine their verbal communication to convey messages with clarity, empathy, and professionalism, fostering productive and meaningful connections in their professional endeavors.

- Non-verbal Communication: Body Language and Dress Code

Non-verbal Communication: Body Language and Dress Code.

Non-verbal communication plays a crucial role in professional interactions, influencing how messages are perceived, relationships are built, and impressions are formed in the workplace. Body language and dress code are key components of non-verbal communication that convey important cues about an individual's demeanor, attitude, and professionalism.

Understanding and effectively utilizing non-verbal communication can significantly impact one's success and effectiveness in professional environments. This comprehensive note explores the significance of body language and dress code in non-verbal communication for professionals and offers insights into how to optimize these aspects for impactful interpersonal exchanges.

Body Language in Professional Settings:

1. **Posture:** Maintaining an upright posture conveys confidence, attentiveness, and authority.

2. **Eye Contact**: Establishing and maintaining eye contact indicates

engagement, sincerity, and active listening.

3. **Gestures:** Using gestures that are natural, purposeful, and appropriate to emphasize points and enhance communication.

4. **Facial Expressions:** Displaying genuine and expressive facial emotions that align with the message being conveyed.

5. **Handshake:** Offering a firm and professional handshake signifies confidence and establishes a positive first impression.

Dress Code and Professional Appearance

1. **Professional Attire:** Dressing appropriately for the workplace, reflecting

the organization's culture, industry norms, and standards of professionalism.

2. Grooming: Maintaining good personal hygiene and grooming practices to present a well-kept and professional appearance.

3. Accessories: Choosing suitable accessories that complement attire without being distracting or overly flashy.

4. Fit and Tailoring: Ensuring clothing fits well and is tailored appropriately to convey a polished and put-together look.

5. Personal Style: Infusing personal style into professional attire while adhering to the organization's dress code guidelines.

Importance of Body Language and Dress Code in Professional Environments:

1. Credibility and Trust: Positive body language and professional attire foster credibility and trust with colleagues, clients, and stakeholders.

2. Professionalism: Non-verbal cues signal professionalism, attention to detail, and respect for the workplace environment.

3. First Impressions: Strong body language and appropriate dress create favorable first impressions, setting the tone for successful interactions.

4. Communication Enhancement: Non-verbal cues complement verbal communication, enhancing the clarity and impact of messages.

5. Relationship Building: Body language and attire contribute to relationship-building efforts, creating rapport and fostering positive connections.

Strategies to Optimize Non-verbal Communication: Body Language and Dress Code:

1. Self-Awareness: Being mindful of one's body language, gestures, and attire to convey desired impressions and messages.

2. Training and Development: Participating in training programs or workshops to enhance non-verbal communication skills.

3. Feedback: Seeking feedback from peers, mentors, or supervisors on body language and dress code to improve professional presence.

4. Role Models: Observing and learning from successful professionals who exhibit strong non-verbal communication skills and professional appearance.

5. Continuous Improvement: Engaging in regular self-assessment and reflection to refine and adapt non-verbal communication strategies for ongoing improvement.

Conclusion

Non-verbal communication, encompassing body language and dress code, plays a significant role in how professionals are perceived and the effectiveness of their interactions in the workplace. By paying attention to body language cues, such as posture, gestures, and eye contact, and aligning dress choices with professional standards and organizational culture, professionals can enhance their credibility, build rapport, and make a positive impact in professional settings. Improving non-verbal communication skills through self-awareness, training, feedback, and continuous refinement can lead to more effective communication, stronger relationships, and heightened success in navigating the complexities of today's professional environments.

Written Communication: Emails, Reports, and Documentation

Written communication plays a vital role in today's business environment, with emails, reports, and documentation being essential components of effective communication. Here is a comprehensive overview of each:

1. Emails:

Purpose: Email is commonly used for quick, informal communication within and outside an organization.

Features: Emails are efficient, cost-effective, and allow for easy dissemination of information.

Best Practices: Be clear, concise, and professional in your emails. Use proper grammar and punctuation, and consider the tone and audience when writing.

Importance: Emails serve as a record of communication, making it essential to maintain professionalism and clarity.

2. **Reports**:

Purpose: Reports are formal documents that convey information, analysis, and recommendations on a specific topic or issue.

Features: Reports are structured documents with headings, subheadings, and a formal tone. They often include an introduction, body, conclusions, and recommendations.

Types: There are various types of reports such as analytical reports, research reports, feasibility reports, and more.

Best Practices: Plan and outline your report before writing, use data and evidence to support your points, and ensure the report is well-organized and easy to follow.

3. Documentation:

Purpose: Documentation encompasses a range of written materials such as policies, procedures, manuals, and guidelines within an organization.

Features: Documentation ensures consistency, efficiency, and clarity in processes and operations. It helps in training new employees, standardizing practices, and providing reference materials.

Best Practices: Keep documentation up-to-date, use clear language and visuals where necessary, and ensure easy accessibility for all stakeholders.

Importance: Good documentation is crucial for knowledge sharing, compliance with regulations, and maintaining organizational effectiveness.

In conclusion, effective written communication through emails, reports, and documentation is essential for conveying information, building relationships, making informed decisions, and ensuring organizational success. By following best practices and understanding the specific requirements of each form of written communication, individuals and organizations can enhance their communication effectiveness and achieve their goals.

Listening Skills: The Key to Effective Communication

Listening skills play a fundamental role in effective communication. Here is a comprehensive overview of the importance of listening skills in communication:

1. Active Listening:

Definition: Active listening involves fully concentrating on what is being said, understanding the information, and responding thoughtfully.

Importance: Active listening shows respect, builds trust, and helps in comprehending the speaker's perspective accurately.

Techniques: Techniques like maintaining eye contact, nodding, paraphrasing, and asking clarifying questions enhance active listening.

2. Empathy and Understanding:

Empathy: Empathetic listening involves understanding and sharing the feelings of the speaker.

Benefits: Empathetic listening fosters stronger relationships, resolves conflicts, and promotes a positive communication environment.

Techniques: Reflecting emotions, validating feelings, and offering support demonstrate empathetic listening.

3. Nonverbal Cues:

Body Language: Paying attention to nonverbal cues such as facial expressions, gestures, and posture enhances understanding and improves communication.

Importance: Nonverbal cues provide essential context and help in interpreting the speaker's message accurately.

4. Avoiding Distractions:

Focus: Minimize distractions like phones, computers, or other interruptions to maintain focus on the speaker.

Importance: Distractions hinder effective listening and can lead to misunderstandings and miscommunication.

5. Feedback and Clarification:

Feedback: Providing feedback and seeking clarification during conversations ensures mutual understanding.

Importance: Feedback helps in confirming understanding, addressing any misconceptions, and fostering open communication.

6. Benefits of Effective Listening:

Improved Relationships: Effective listening strengthens relationships, builds trust, and enhances collaboration.

Conflict Resolution: Good listening skills aid in resolving conflicts, improving negotiation, and reaching mutually beneficial solutions.

Enhanced Problem-Solving: Listening attentively leads to better decision-making, problem-solving, and increased productivity.

In conclusion, listening skills are crucial for effective communication as they enhance understanding, build trust, and foster positive relationships. By practicing active listening, showing empathy, paying attention to nonverbal cues, avoiding distractions, and providing feedback, individuals can significantly improve their communication abilities and achieve greater success in personal and professional interactions.

Chapter 4: Interpersonal Skills and Teamwork

Interpersonal skills and teamwork are essential for success in both personal and professional settings. Here is a comprehensive overview of the importance of interpersonal skills and teamwork:

1. Interpersonal Skills:

Definition: Interpersonal skills are the abilities to communicate, interact, and collaborate effectively with others.

Key Skills: Active listening, empathy, conflict resolution, assertiveness, and emotional intelligence are crucial interpersonal skills.

Importance: Strong interpersonal skills enable individuals to build and maintain relationships, resolve conflicts, and work well with others.

2. Communication:

Effective Communication: Clear and open communication is vital for expressing ideas, sharing feedback, and understanding others.

Nonverbal Communication: Paying attention to nonverbal cues, such as body language and tone of voice, enhances communication effectiveness.

3. Empathy and Emotional Intelligence:

Empathy: Understanding and sharing the feelings of others fosters trust, cooperation, and stronger relationships.

Emotional Intelligence: The ability to regulate emotions, empathize with others, and navigate social interactions positively is key to strong interpersonal skills.

4. Conflict Resolution:

Conflict Management: Resolving conflicts through effective communication, understanding different perspectives, and seeking mutually beneficial solutions is essential for successful teamwork.

Negotiation Skills: Negotiating compromises and finding common ground help in resolving conflicts and reaching agreements.

5. Teamwork:

Definition: Teamwork involves collaboration, cooperation, and collective effort to achieve a common goal or objective.

Benefits: Teamwork enhances creativity, innovation, problem-solving, and productivity.

Roles and Responsibilities: Clearly defining roles, setting goals, and fostering a sense of ownership among team members are vital for effective teamwork.

6. Leadership and Followership:

Leadership: Effective leaders inspire, motivate, and guide team members towards shared goals.

Followership: Active participation, support for team goals, and collaboration with team members contribute to successful teamwork.

7. Communication and Feedback:

Open Communication: Encouraging open dialogue, sharing information, and providing feedback promote effective teamwork.

Constructive Feedback: Offering constructive feedback, recognizing achievements, and addressing concerns constructively strengthen team dynamics.

In conclusion, developing strong interpersonal skills, including effective communication, empathy, conflict resolution, and teamwork abilities, is essential for building positive relationships, fostering collaboration, and achieving success in both personal and professional endeavors. By cultivating these skills and embracing teamwork principles, individuals can contribute meaningfully to team efforts, drive organizational success, and create a positive work environment conducive to growth and innovation.

- Building Productive Relationships

Building productive relationships in business professionalism is a cornerstone of success in the modern business world. Here is a comprehensive overview of how to build and maintain productive relationships in a professional setting:

1. Communication:

Clear Communication: Ensure communication is clear, concise, and tailored to the audience to avoid misunderstandings.

Active Listening: Practice active listening by giving your full attention, asking clarifying questions, and showing genuine interest in others' perspectives.

Feedback: Provide constructive feedback, acknowledge contributions, and address concerns promptly to maintain healthy communication channels.

2. Trust and Integrity:

Reliability: Demonstrate reliability by following through on commitments, meeting deadlines, and being consistent in your actions.

Transparency: Be open and honest in your dealings, disclose relevant information, and maintain confidentiality to build trust with colleagues and clients.

Ethical Behavior: Uphold ethical standards, adhere to company policies, and act with integrity in all business interactions to establish credibility and trust.

3. Professionalism:

Professional Demeanor: Present yourself professionally through proper attire, language, and behavior in all business settings.

Respect: Treat others with respect, value diverse perspectives, and maintain a positive attitude even in challenging situations.

Boundaries: Understand and respect professional boundaries, maintain confidentiality, and avoid conflicts of interest to uphold professionalism.

4. Networking:

Building Connections: Actively network with colleagues, industry peers, and potential clients to expand your professional circle and create opportunities for collaboration.

Relationship Building: Invest time in developing meaningful relationships, building rapport, and connecting on a personal level to foster trust and mutual respect.

Maintaining Relationships: Stay in touch with contacts, show appreciation for their support, and offer assistance when needed to nurture long-lasting professional relationships.

5. Conflict Resolution:

Open Communication: Address conflicts directly, express concerns respectfully, and work towards finding mutually acceptable solutions.

Negotiation Skills: Develop negotiation skills to resolve conflicts, reach compromises, and maintain positive relationships in challenging situations.

Seeking Resolution: Approach conflicts with a solution-oriented mindset, focus on common goals, and seek input from all parties involved to achieve resolution effectively.

In conclusion, building productive relationships in a professional business environment requires effective communication, mutual trust, professionalism, networking, and conflict resolution skills. By cultivating these attributes and fostering positive interactions with others, individuals can create a collaborative and supportive work environment, strengthen partnerships, and drive success in their professional endeavors.

- Conflict Resolution and Negotiation

Conflict resolution and negotiation are essential skills in both personal and professional settings. Here is a comprehensive overview of conflict resolution and negotiation:

1. Conflict Resolution:

Definition: Conflict resolution involves addressing disagreements or disputes in a constructive manner to reach a mutually acceptable solution.

Importance: Effective conflict resolution promotes understanding, strengthens relationships, and fosters a positive work environment.

Approaches: Common conflict resolution approaches include collaboration, compromise, accommodation, avoidance, and competition.

Steps: The typical steps in conflict resolution include identifying the issue, understanding each party's perspective, exploring solutions, and reaching a resolution through dialogue and cooperation.

2. Key Skills for Conflict Resolution:

Active Listening: Listening attentively to others' viewpoints to understand their concerns.

Empathy: Putting oneself in the other person's shoes to understand their feelings and perspective.

Communication: Expressing thoughts and feelings clearly and respectfully.

Problem-Solving: Collaborating to find mutually beneficial solutions that address underlying issues.

3. Negotiation:

Definition: Negotiation is a process in which two or more parties seek to find a mutually acceptable solution to a conflict or disagreement.

Importance: Effective negotiation skills are essential in business, personal relationships, and everyday interactions.

Types: Negotiation can be distributive (win-lose) or integrative (win-win) depending on the goals and approach of the parties involved.

Strategies: Common negotiation strategies include identifying interests, setting priorities, maintaining flexibility, and seeking creative solutions.

4. Key Skills for Negotiation:

Preparation: Gathering information, setting objectives, and understanding the other party's perspective.

Effective Communication: Clearly articulating your position, actively listening to the other party, and building rapport to facilitate understanding.

Problem-Solving: Identifying common ground, exploring options, and finding creative solutions to reach a mutually beneficial agreement.

Emotional Intelligence: Managing emotions, staying composed under pressure, and maintaining a positive rapport during negotiations.

5. Negotiation Techniques:

BATNA (Best Alternative to a Negotiated Agreement): Understanding your alternatives if negotiations fail.

ZOPA (Zone of Possible Agreement): Identifying the potential range of agreement that is acceptable to both parties.

Concessions: Offering and accepting concessions to move negotiations forward and reach a compromise.

Closing the Deal: Formally agreeing on the terms, documenting the agreement, and following up to ensure implementation.

In conclusion, conflict resolution and negotiation skills are crucial for managing conflicts, resolving disputes, and reaching mutually beneficial agreements. By developing effective communication, problem-solving, and negotiation skills, individuals can navigate conflicts successfully, build stronger relationships, and achieve positive outcomes in various personal and professional contexts.

Collaborating in a Team Environment

Collaboration in a team environment is essential for achieving shared goals, fostering creativity, and maximizing productivity. Here is a comprehensive overview of collaborating in a team environment:

1. Definition of Collaboration:

Collaboration: Collaboration is the process of working together with others to achieve a common goal, solve problems, and generate ideas through shared effort and collective input.

Key Elements: Collaboration involves communication, trust, mutual respect, flexibility, and a commitment to teamwork.

2. Benefits of Collaboration:

Diverse Perspectives: Collaborating with team members from different backgrounds and expertise leads to a more comprehensive understanding and innovative solutions.

Increased Productivity: Sharing responsibilities, expertise, and resources within a team environment boosts efficiency and productivity.

Improved Decision-Making: Collaborative decision-making allows for a wider range of input, leading to well-rounded decisions and outcomes.

Enhanced Creativity: Combining diverse perspectives and brainstorming ideas collectively sparks creativity and innovative solutions.

3. **Key Principles of Collaborating in a Team Environment:**

Open Communication: Encouraging open dialogue, active listening, and sharing of ideas fosters a collaborative environment.

Mutual Respect: Valuing team members' contributions, skills, and perspectives creates a foundation of respect and trust.

Shared Goals: Establishing clear goals, roles, and expectations ensures alignment and focus within the team.

Conflict Resolution: Addressing conflicts constructively and seeking solutions that benefit the team as a whole promotes a positive team environment.

4. **Effective Collaboration Techniques:**

Team Building Activities: Engaging in team-building exercises, retreats, and workshops helps foster trust, communication, and collaboration among team members.

Regular Communication: Holding regular team meetings, check-ins, and progress updates ensures that everyone is informed and aligned.

Utilizing Technology: Leveraging collaborative tools, project management software, and communication platforms facilitates seamless interaction and sharing of information among team members.

Feedback and Reflection: Providing feedback, reflecting on team dynamics, and evaluating processes and outcomes enhance collaboration and continuous improvement.

5. Roles and Responsibilities in Collaborative Teams:

Role Clarity: Clearly defining roles, responsibilities, and expectations within the team prevents misunderstandings and promotes accountability.

Task Allocation: Assigning tasks based on each team member's strengths, skills, and interests optimizes efficiency and productivity.

Support and Encouragement: Offering support, encouragement, and recognition for team members' efforts and achievements motivates and strengthens collaboration.

In conclusion, effective collaboration in a team environment requires open communication, mutual respect, shared goals, and effective conflict resolution. By fostering a culture of collaboration, leveraging diverse perspectives, and implementing effective teamwork strategies and techniques, teams can harness collective strengths, drive innovation, and achieve greater success in their endeavors.

- Leadership and Influence

Leadership and influence are critical aspects of guiding and inspiring individuals and teams towards common goals.

Here is a comprehensive overview of leadership and influence:

1. Leadership:

Definition: Leadership involves setting a clear vision, inspiring others, making strategic decisions, and fostering growth and development within an organization or team.

Leadership Styles: Different leadership styles include autocratic, democratic, transformational, servant, and situational leadership, each with its unique approach to guiding and motivating others.

Traits of Effective Leaders: Effective leaders possess traits such as integrity, empathy, vision, decisiveness, resilience, and the ability to inspire and empower others.

Impact of Leadership: Strong leadership influences organizational culture, employee engagement, productivity, and overall success.

2. Influence:

Definition: Influence is the ability to affect the thoughts, beliefs, and actions of others, leading to desired outcomes or decisions.

Sources of Influence: Influence can stem from expertise, authority, relationships, persuasion, negotiation skills, and the ability to inspire and motivate others.

Types of Influence: Positive influence involves inspiring and guiding others towards positive actions, while negative influence can manipulate or coerce others for personal gain.

Effective Influence Strategies: Building trust, establishing credibility, maintaining open communication, and leading by example are key strategies for effective influence.

3. Leadership vs. Management:

Leadership: Leadership focuses on setting direction, inspiring others, empowering team members, and fostering innovation and growth.

Management: Management involves planning, organizing, coordinating, and controlling resources to achieve specific goals and objectives within an organization.

4. Key Aspects of Effective Leadership:

Vision and Strategy: Articulating a compelling vision, setting clear goals, and developing strategic plans to guide the team or organization.

Communication: Communicating effectively, listening actively, and fostering open dialogue to ensure clarity and alignment.

Decision-making: Making sound and timely decisions based on data, input from stakeholders, and consideration of potential outcomes.

Empowerment: Empowering team members, delegating responsibilities, and providing opportunities for growth and development.

Adaptability: Adapting to change, being open to feedback, learning from failures, and continuously improving leadership practices.

5. Building Influence:

Building Relationships: Establishing strong relationships, displaying empathy, and understanding the needs and motivations of others.

Leading by Example: Demonstrating integrity, authenticity, and the values you wish to instill in others.

Inspiring Others: Motivating and inspiring team members through shared vision, recognition, and support.

In conclusion, effective leadership and influence are essential for guiding individuals and teams towards shared goals, fostering collaboration, and driving organizational success. By cultivating leadership skills, leveraging influence strategically, and inspiring others through positive actions and behaviors, individuals can create a positive impact, foster growth, and achieve desired outcomes in personal and professional contexts.

Chapter 5: Time Management and Productivity

Time management and productivity are crucial skills in today's fast-paced and demanding work environments. Here is a comprehensive overview of time management and productivity:

1. Time Management:

Definition: Time management is the process of planning, organizing, and prioritizing tasks and activities to make the most efficient use of time.

Benefits: Effective time management leads to increased productivity, reduced stress, improved work-life balance, and better overall performance.

 - *Key Principles*:

Setting Goals: Establish clear goals and objectives to guide your daily activities.

Prioritization: Identify and prioritize tasks based on importance and deadlines.

Planning: Create daily, weekly, or monthly schedules to allocate time for tasks and activities.

Avoiding Procrastination: Tackle tasks promptly and avoid delaying important work.

Time Tracking: Monitor how you spend your time to identify areas for improvement.

2. Productivity:

Definition: Productivity refers to the efficiency in which tasks and goals are accomplished, maximizing output while minimizing input (time, resources, effort).

Improving Productivity:

Effective Planning: Break down tasks into smaller, manageable components and set realistic deadlines.

Eliminating Distractions: Minimize interruptions, such as emails, phone calls, and social media, to maintain focus.

Utilizing Tools: Make use of productivity tools like calendars, task managers, and project management software to streamline work processes.

Delegating: Delegate tasks to others when possible to free up time for high-priority work.

Continuous Learning: Stay updated on best practices, techniques, and tools to enhance productivity.

Self-Care: Prioritize self-care, including adequate rest, breaks, and physical activity, to maintain energy and focus.

3. Time Management Techniques:

Pomodoro Technique: Break work into intervals (e.g., 25 minutes of focused work followed by a short break) to enhance productivity and focus.

Eisenhower Matrix: Prioritize tasks based on urgency and importance to determine what should be tackled first.

Time Blocking: Allocate specific blocks of time for different tasks and activities to maintain focus and avoid multitasking.

Batching: Group similar tasks together to minimize context switching and improve efficiency.

Goal Setting: Establish SMART (Specific, Measurable, Achievable, Relevant, Time-bound) goals to provide clear direction and motivation.

4. Overcoming Time Management Challenges:

Procrastination: Identify the root causes of procrastination and implement strategies to overcome it, such as breaking tasks into smaller steps or setting deadlines.

Overcommitment: Learn to say no, set boundaries, and prioritize tasks to avoid taking on more than you can handle.

Lack of Focus: Practice mindfulness, eliminate distractions, and create a conducive work environment to enhance concentration.

Poor Planning: Develop strong planning skills, allocate sufficient time for tasks, and adjust schedules as needed to improve time management.

In conclusion, mastering time management and improving productivity are essential skills for achieving personal and professional success. By implementing effective time management techniques, prioritizing tasks, minimizing distractions, and maintaining work-life balance, individuals can optimize their productivity, accomplish goals efficiently, and reduce stress in today's demanding work environment.

- Setting Priorities and Goals

Setting priorities and goals is essential for achieving success and staying focused in both personal and professional life. Here is a comprehensive note on the importance and strategies for setting priorities and goals:

Importance of Setting Priorities and Goals:

1. **Clarity**: Having well-defined priorities and goals provides clarity on what needs to be done and helps in avoiding distractions.

2. **Motivation**: Goals serve as a source of motivation, providing a clear target to work towards and a sense of achievement upon completion.

3. **Time Management**: Prioritizing tasks helps in effective time management, ensuring that the most important and urgent tasks are addressed first.

4. **Focus**: Setting priorities helps in maintaining focus on what truly matters, reducing the likelihood of getting overwhelmed by a multitude of tasks.

5. Measurable Progress: Goals provide a benchmark for measuring progress and success, allowing for adjustments and improvements along the way.

Strategies for Setting Priorities and Goals:

1. Identify Values: Start by identifying your core values and long-term aspirations, as they will guide you in setting meaningful goals.

2. SMART Objectives: Ensure that your objectives are Time-bound, Relevant, Specific, Measurable, and Achievable. This ensures clarity and accountability.

3. Prioritization Matrix: Use tools like the Eisenhower Matrix to categorize tasks based on urgency and importance, helping you prioritize effectively.

4. Break Down Goals: Large goals can be intimidating, so break them down into smaller, manageable tasks with deadlines to track progress.

5. Regular Review: Regularly review and reassess your priorities and goals to stay aligned with your values and adapt to changing circumstances.

Tips for Effective Goal Setting:

1. Be Realistic: Set goals that are challenging yet attainable, considering your resources and constraints.

2. Stay Flexible: Be open to adapting your goals as needed based on feedback and changing circumstances.

3. Celebrate Achievements: Celebrate your accomplishments along the way to stay motivated and reinforce positive behavior.

4. Seek Feedback: Share your goals with trusted individuals who can provide feedback and support your journey.

5. Self-Reflection: Take time to reflect on your progress, learn from setbacks, and adjust your approach accordingly.

In conclusion, setting priorities and goals is a critical step towards personal and professional growth. By defining what truly matters to you, setting clear objectives, and staying focused on your path, you can maximize your productivity, motivation, and overall success.

Managing Workload and Deadlines

Managing workload and deadlines effectively is crucial for maintaining productivity, reducing stress, and achieving optimal results in both personal and professional endeavors. Here is a comprehensive note on strategies for managing workload and deadlines:

Importance of Managing Workload and Deadlines:

1. **Productivity:** Effective workload management ensures tasks are completed efficiently, maximizing productivity.

2. **Stress Reduction**: Properly managed workloads and deadlines help reduce

stress levels by avoiding last-minute rushes and overwhelming workloads.

3. Quality of Work: Managing workload and deadlines allows for adequate time to focus on tasks, resulting in higher quality work.

4. Accountability: Setting and meeting deadlines fosters accountability and reliability in personal and professional relationships.

5. Time Management: Efficient workload and deadline management aids in effective time management, allowing for a balanced work-life schedule.

Strategies for Managing Workload and Deadlines:

1. **Prioritize Tasks**: Use methods like the Eisenhower Matrix to prioritize tasks based on urgency and importance.

2. **Set Realistic Expectations**: Be realistic about what can be accomplished within a given timeframe to avoid overloading yourself.

3. **Break Tasks into Smaller Steps:** Break down larger tasks into smaller, manageable steps to prevent feeling overwhelmed.

4. **Use Time Management Tools**: Utilize tools like calendars, task management apps, and to-do lists to stay organized and on track.

5. Establish Deadlines: Set clear deadlines for tasks and projects, and consider using reminders to stay on schedule.

Tips for Managing Workload and Deadlines Effectively:

1. Time Blocking: Allocate specific time blocks for different tasks and avoid multitasking to enhance focus and efficiency.

2. Avoid Procrastination: Address tasks promptly to prevent last-minute rushes and ensure timely completion.

3. Delegate Tasks: Delegate tasks when possible to lighten your workload and increase overall efficiency.

4.   **Communicate**:   Keep   open communication with team members or colleagues regarding workload and deadlines to prevent misunderstandings.

5. **Self-Care**: Prioritize self-care practices such as exercise, adequate sleep, and breaks to maintain overall well-being and productivity.

In conclusion, effective workload and deadline management are essential skills for success in any field. By prioritizing tasks, setting realistic goals, utilizing time management tools, and practicing proper self-care, individuals can improve productivity, reduce stress, and achieve optimal results in their personal and professional lives.

Overcoming Procrastination

Overcoming procrastination is a common challenge faced by many individuals, hindering productivity and causing unnecessary stress. Here is a comprehensive note on understanding procrastination and strategies to overcome it:

Understanding Procrastination:

1. **Definition**: Procrastination refers to the act of delaying or postponing tasks or activities, often to the point of causing negative consequences.

2. **Causes**: Procrastination can be attributed to various factors, such as fear of failure, lack of motivation,

perfectionism, task aversion, or poor time management skills.

3. **Effects**: Procrastination can lead to increased stress, reduced productivity, missed deadlines, diminished quality of work, and overall dissatisfaction with one's accomplishments.

Strategies to Overcome Procrastination:

1. **Identify the Root Cause**: Reflect on the reasons behind your procrastination and address underlying issues, whether they are related to fear, lack of interest, or overwhelm.

2. **Set Clear Goals**: Establish specific, measurable, achievable, relevant, and time-bound (SMART) goals to provide clarity and motivation for completing tasks.

3. Break Tasks Down: Divide larger tasks into smaller, more manageable steps to prevent feeling overwhelmed and make progress more achievable.

4. Create a Routine: Establish a daily or weekly routine that includes dedicated time for tasks, breaks, and self-care activities to maintain a sense of structure and accountability.

5. Utilize Time Management Techniques: Employ time management tools like calendars, to-do lists, prioritization methods, and time-blocking to organize tasks and improve productivity.

6. Practice the Two-Minute Rule: Start with a task that takes just two minutes to complete. This can help build momentum and alleviate the inertia that leads to procrastination.

7. Reward Yourself: Implement a reward system where you treat yourself upon completing tasks or reaching milestones to reinforce positive behavior.

8. Eliminate Distractions: Identify and minimize distractions in your environment, such as social media, noise, or clutter, to maintain focus and concentration.

9. Seek Accountability: Share your goals and progress with a friend, colleague, or mentor who can hold you accountable and provide support and encouragement.

10. Practice Self-Compassion: Be kind to yourself and acknowledge that occasional setbacks are normal. Recognize your mistakes as teaching moments and seize the chance to improve.

In conclusion, overcoming procrastination requires self-awareness, discipline, and effective strategies to combat avoidance behaviors and enhance productivity. By understanding the root causes of procrastination, setting clear goals, implementing time management techniques, and practicing self-care, individuals can break the cycle of procrastination and achieve success in their personal and professional pursuits.

Tools and Techniques for Efficiency

Improving efficiency is crucial for maximizing productivity and achieving optimal results in various aspects of life. Here is a comprehensive note on tools and techniques that can help enhance efficiency:

Efficiency Tools:

1. **Project Management Software**: Tools like Trello, Asana, or Monday.com help

organize tasks, track progress, assign responsibilities, and collaborate with team members efficiently.

2. Time Tracking Apps: Apps such as Toggl or RescueTime help monitor how time is spent, identify time-wasters, and optimize workflows for increased productivity.

3. Calendar Apps: Platforms like Google Calendar or Microsoft Outlook assist in scheduling meetings, setting reminders, and managing appointments to structure your day effectively.

4. Note-Taking Tools: Applications like Evernote, Microsoft OneNote, or Notion help capture ideas, organize information, and collaborate on notes for improved information management.

5. Communication Tools: Platforms like Slack, Microsoft Teams, or Zoom facilitate seamless communication, file sharing, and collaboration among team members, enhancing workflow efficiency.

Efficiency Techniques:

1. Pareto Principle (80/20 Rule): Focus on the 20% of tasks that deliver 80% of results to prioritize effectively and maximize productivity.

2. Batching Tasks: Group similar tasks together and tackle them in batches to minimize context switching and increase focus and efficiency.

3. Eisenhower Matrix: Categorize tasks into urgent, important, non-urgent, and non-important categories to prioritize tasks based on importance and urgency.

4. Pomodoro Technique: Break work into intervals (usually 25 minutes of focused work followed by a short break) to boost concentration and maintain productivity.

5. Kanban Method: Visualize workflows using boards with columns like "To-Do," "In Progress," and "Done" to track tasks and improve work efficiency.

6. GTD (Getting Things Done): Implement the GTD method by capturing, clarifying, organizing, reviewing, and engaging with tasks to enhance productivity and reduce mental clutter.

7. Single-Tasking: Focus on one task at a time to increase concentration, reduce distractions, and complete tasks more efficiently.

8. Outsourcing and Delegation: Delegate tasks that can be handled by others or consider outsourcing certain responsibilities to free up time for high-priority tasks.

9. Continuous Learning: Stay updated with industry trends, technologies, and best practices through continuous learning to enhance skills and efficiency.

10. Self-Care: Prioritize rest, exercise, healthy eating, and mindfulness practices to maintain physical and mental well-being, which is essential for sustained efficiency.

In conclusion, utilizing tools and techniques for efficiency can significantly improve productivity, time management, and overall performance. By incorporating these tools and techniques into daily routines, individuals can streamline workflows, reduce inefficiencies, and achieve their goals with greater effectiveness.

Chapter 6: Digital Professionalism and Online Etiquette

Digital Professionalism and Online Etiquette embody the standards, behaviors, and ethics we observe when interacting in the digital world. As our personal and professional lives continue to integrate with digital platforms—ranging from emails and social media to professional networking sites and virtual workspaces—understanding and practicing digital professionalism and online etiquette become increasingly crucial. This comprehensive note will explore key aspects and provide guidance on maintaining professionalism and etiquette online.

Understanding Digital Professionalism:

Digital Professionalism refers to the way individuals present themselves and interact with others in a digital environment in a manner that is respectful, ethical, and in line with the expected norms of their profession or social context. It encompasses various elements, including communication style, privacy management, digital footprint, and online behavior.

Key Components of Digital Professionalism:

Privacy Management: Understanding and managing the privacy settings on your digital platforms to protect personal information and maintain professional boundaries.

Digital Footprint: Being aware of the information about yourself that is available online and how it reflects on your professionalism. This includes content you post and interactions with others' content.

Ethical Conduct: Adhering to ethical standards in professional interactions, respecting confidentiality, and avoiding conflicts of interest.

Professional Communication: Ensuring that communication is clear, respectful, and appropriate for the audience and context.

Online Etiquette

Online Etiquette, often referred to as "netiquette," involves the informal guidelines and norms governing polite behavior online. These guidelines help facilitate respectful and constructive interactions in digital spaces.

Essential Elements of Online Etiquette:
Respect and Civility: Treating others with respect, acknowledging differing opinions, and communicating politely.

Responsiveness: Responding to professional communications in a timely manner, considering differences in time zones and schedules.

Clarity and Brevity: Keeping communication clear and to the point to avoid misunderstandings. This may include using appropriate language, avoiding jargon when possible, and being concise.

Digital Presence: Being mindful of how you present yourself online, including profile pictures, bios, and the content you share.

Confidentiality: Keeping sensitive information private, sharing only what is necessary and appropriate in a given context.

Implementing Digital Professionalism and Online Etiquette:
Implementing digital professionalism and online etiquette requires ongoing attention to how you engage with others online and how you manage your digital presence. Here are a few practical tips:

1. Regularly Review Digital Footprint: Periodically Google yourself to monitor what information is publicly available about you online.

2. Maintain Privacy Settings: Regularly update your privacy settings on social media and other platforms to control who can see your information and posts.

3. Professional Profiles: Ensure your professional profiles, especially on networking sites like LinkedIn, are complete, up-to-date, and reflect your best self.

4. Mind Your Manners: Treat online interactions with the same courtesy and professionalism you would in person.

5. Stay Informed: Keep abreast of changing norms and expectations in digital professionalism and online etiquette.

By cultivating digital professionalism and observing online etiquette, you not only protect and enhance your professional reputation but also contribute to healthier, more respectful digital environments for everyone.

Managing Digital Footprint

Managing your digital footprint is crucial in today's digital age, where vast amounts of personal and professional information are shared online. A digital footprint is essentially the trail of data you leave behind while using the internet. This includes things you post about yourself, as well as what others post about you and any data collected by websites and applications you use. Managing this digital trail carefully is important for protecting your privacy, maintaining your online reputation, and ensuring your personal security. This comprehensive note will provide insights and strategies for effectively managing your digital footprint.

Understanding Your Digital Footprint:

Your digital footprint can be divided into two main types: Active and Passive.

Active Digital Footprint: This consists of the information you deliberately share online, such as social media posts, blogs, comments, and other online interactions.

Passive Digital Footprint: This footprint is created when information is collected about you without you actively sharing it.

It includes data collected by websites about your browsing habits, search history, and online purchases, among others.

Strategies for Managing Your Digital Footprint:

Audit Your Online Presence.

Make an online presence audit your first step. Search for yourself on various search engines and note what information about you is publicly accessible. Don't forget to check images and videos as well. This can give you a good idea of the magnitude of your digital footprint.

Adjust Privacy Settings:

Make sure you frequently check and modify the privacy settings on your other online accounts, including social media. Decide who you want to share your information with and adjust your settings to reflect that. Be wary of default settings, as they may not provide the level of privacy you expect.

Be Mindful of What You Share:

Before posting anything online, consider its potential impact on your privacy and online reputation. Ask yourself if it's something you wouldn't mind being permanently accessible online. Be particularly cautious with personal information that could be used for identity theft, such as your address, phone number, and date of birth.

Regularly Update and Secure Your Accounts:

Make sure all of your online accounts have strong, distinct passwords, and change them frequently. To manage your passwords, think about utilizing a password manager. Enable two-factor authentication whenever it is possible to further enhance security.

Educate Yourself on Digital Rights and Policies:

Understand the terms of service and privacy policies of the platforms you use. Be aware of your digital rights, including the right to be forgotten, which allows you to request the deletion of your information from a company's records in certain circumstances.

Clean Up Your Digital Footprint

Consider removing outdated or unwanted content from the internet. This may involve deleting old social media posts, requesting website administrators to remove information about you, or utilizing services that specialize in online reputation management.

Monitor Your Digital Footprint:
Make it a habit to periodically check your digital footprint. Set up Google alerts for your name to monitor new mentions of you online. Regularly review and clean up your online presence to ensure it reflects how you want to be seen.

Be Selective with Apps and Services:
Before downloading an app or signing up for a service, consider what personal information it requires and how it will be used. Apps that ask for unnecessary permissions should be avoided.

Conclusion

In an era where online activities are intricately linked with personal and professional identities, managing your digital footprint is not optional—it's essential. By taking proactive steps to understand, monitor, and control your online presence, you can protect your privacy, secure your personal data, and shape your digital reputation in a way that reflects your true self. Remember, the digital footprint you leave is a reflection of your personal brand, and managing it wisely is key to navigating the digital world safely and effectively.

Email Etiquette and Online Communication

Email etiquette and online communication are fundamental in today's digital world, where most of our professional and personal conversations happen over the internet. Being fluent in the unspoken rules of email and online dialogs can make significant differences in how your messages are received and perceived. Here's a comprehensive note covering the essential aspects of email etiquette and online communication:

The Basics of Email Etiquette:

1. Subject Line Clarity:

- The subject line should be concise and informative, providing the recipient with a clear idea of the email content.

2. Professional Salutations:

- Begin with a proper greeting e.g., "Dear [Name]," or "Hello [Name]," using titles when appropriate.

3. Concise and Clear Messaging:

- Keep your emails brief yet comprehensive. Be direct and to the point, ensuring that your message is easily understood.

4. Proper Formatting:

- Use paragraphs to break up text, bullet points for lists, and bold or italics for emphasis (sparingly) to make your email easier to read.

5. Polite Language:

- Maintain a polite and professional tone throughout your email, even when discussing negative aspects.

6. Proofreading:

- Always check your email for grammatical mistakes and typos before sending. This reflects your attention to detail and respect for the recipient.

7. Sign-Offs:

- End with a polite closure, such as "Best regards," "Sincerely," followed by your name and, optionally, your contact information.

Online Communication Norms:

1. Respecting Time Zones:

- When working with people in different time zones, be mindful of sending messages during their local business hours, when possible.

2. Use of Emojis:

- In professional settings, use emojis sparingly and only if you know the recipient well enough to understand how they'll be received.

3. Responsiveness:

- Aim to respond to emails and online messages in a timely manner, even if only to acknowledge receipt and provide a timeframe for a detailed reply.

4. Confidentiality and Privacy:

- Be cautious about sharing sensitive or personal information over email or online platforms. Always ensure you're communicating over secure channels.

5. Digital Awareness:

- Remember that digital communications lack tone and non-verbal cues. What you intend as humor or sarcasm might not be perceived as such.

6. Thread and Context Awareness:

- When responding to an ongoing email thread, ensure your reply is relevant to the current line of discussion and that you're addressing the correct recipients.

7. Attachment Etiquette:

- When sending attachments, mention them in your email, ensure they are appropriately sized, or use file sharing services for larger documents.

Advanced Tips:

Personalization and Empathy:

Understanding and acknowledging the recipient's perspective or current workload can go a long way in fostering positive relationships.

Cultural Sensitivity:

Being aware of and respectful towards the cultural differences in communication styles, formalities, and sensitivities.

Feedback Loops:

Encourage open channels of communication where feedback is welcome, and misunderstandings can be quickly addressed.

Mastering email etiquette and online communication skills not only enhances your professional image but also improves your interactions, leading to more efficient and effective communication. Whether you're corresponding with colleagues, clients, or friends online, these practices are invaluable in navigating the digital communication landscape responsibly and respectfully.

Professionalism on Social Media

Professionalism on social media is crucial for individuals aiming to maintain a positive and respectable online presence, particularly for those using these platforms for career development, networking, or brand representation. As social media blurs the lines between personal and professional spheres, understanding how to navigate these platforms professionally is essential. Here's a comprehensive note on maintaining professionalism on social media:

Understanding the Platform:
1. Platform-Specific Norms:
   - Every social media platform has its own set of norms and expected behaviors.

LinkedIn, for example, is a professional networking site where career achievements and professional discussions predominate, while Instagram may be more casual but still requires a level of professionalism when used for business purposes.

2. Privacy Settings and Audience Segmentation:

- Familiarize yourself with the privacy settings on each platform to control who sees your content. Utilizing features like audience segmentation can help maintain a professional image while still sharing personal moments with a select audience.

Crafting Your Online Presence:

1. Professional Profile:

- Ensure your profile picture and bio reflect your professional image. It's advisable to use a headshot or a logo for business accounts, along with a bio that succinctly describes your professional identity or brand.

2. Consistent Branding:

- For professionals and businesses, maintaining consistent branding across platforms helps in establishing credibility and recognition.

3. Content Creation and Sharing:

- Share valuable content that reflects your expertise, interests, and professional ethos. This can include thoughtful articles, insightful commentary on industry news, or sharing achievements. Balance is key—while it's beneficial to share your successes, also contribute to the community by engaging with and promoting others' work.

Engagement and Communication:

1. Professional Language:

- While social media tends to be more informal, maintaining professional language and decorum is essential. Avoid slang, jargon (unless industry-specific), and anything that could be deemed offensive or unprofessional.

2. Network Building:

- Connect and engage with peers, industry leaders, and potential clients or employers respectfully. Personalized messages when connecting, and thoughtful, constructive comments on others' posts can foster meaningful relationships.

3. Responding to Feedback:

- Whether you receive positive or negative feedback, respond professionally. Thank and engage with positive comments, and approach criticism constructively, viewing it as an opportunity for growth or clarification.

Navigating Controversies and Criticism:

1. Crisis Management:

   - If faced with a social media crisis (e.g., a post that sparks significant negative feedback), address the issue directly and maturely. If necessary, apologize, clarify your stance, or take the discussion offline.

2. Avoiding Public Disputes:

   - Engage in debates respectfully and avoid public disputes. If a conversation turns negative, propose taking the discussion to a private channel or agree to disagree respectfully.

3. Political and Sensitive Topics:

   - Exercise caution when commenting on political or other sensitive issues. While it's important to stand by your values, consider the implications of your public statements on your professional image and relationships.

Continuous Improvement:

Stay Informed:

Keeping abreast of changing social media trends, platform updates, and best practices in digital communication is crucial for maintaining professionalism online.

Self-Audit:

Periodically review your online presence, including the content you've shared and your engagements with others. This can help you refine your strategy and ensure consistency with your professional goals.

Professionalism on social media, much like in traditional settings, revolves around respect, decorum, and engagement that adds value to your network. By thoughtfully managing your online presence, you not only safeguard your personal brand but also open doors to opportunities and meaningful connections in your industry.

Cybersecurity Basics for Professionals

In our increasingly digital world, cybersecurity has become a paramount concern for professionals across all industries. Safeguarding data—be it personal information, sensitive corporate data, or client details—against unauthorized access, theft, or damage, is not just a technical issue but a foundational aspect of professional conduct and responsibility. Here's a comprehensive guide on cybersecurity basics for professionals, outlining key principles, practices, and strategies to enhance your digital security posture.

Understanding Cybersecurity Risks

1. Malware:

- Malicious software, including viruses, worms, and ransomware, designed to disrupt, damage, or gain unauthorized access to systems.

2. Phishing:

- Fraudulent practices, such as sending emails pretending to be from reputable companies, to induce individuals to reveal personal information.

3. Man-in-the-Middle (MitM) Attacks:

- Where attackers intercept and alter communications between two parties without their knowledge.

4. Denial-of-Service (DoS) Attacks:

- Attempts to disrupt service to a network by overwhelming the target with a flood of internet traffic.

5. Data Breaches:

- The unauthorized access and extraction of sensitive, confidential, or protected data.

Key Cybersecurity Practices

1. **Strong Passwords and Authentication Measures:**

- Use complex passwords and enable multi-factor authentication (MFA) wherever possible to strengthen access control.

2. **Regular Software Updates and Patch Management:**

- Keep all software updated to protect against known vulnerabilities, employing automated updates when available.

3. **Secure Wi-Fi Networks:**

- Ensure Wi-Fi networks are secure, encrypted, and hidden. Steer clear of sensitive transactions on public Wi-Fi if you're not using a VPN.

4. Data Encryption:

- Encrypt sensitive data in transit and at rest, reducing the risk of data breaches and ensuring data integrity and confidentiality.

5. Awareness and Training:

- Regularly educate yourself and your team on the latest cybersecurity threats and safe practices, including recognizing phishing emails and safely managing digital records.

6- Make sure backup copies of your data are safely stored and regularly backup your data. This can mitigate the damage in case of data loss or ransomware attacks.

Advanced Cybersecurity Strategies

1. Network Security:

- Use firewalls, intrusion detection systems (IDS), and intrusion prevention systems (IPS) to monitor and protect your network from unauthorized access.

2. Endpoint Protection:

- Secure all endpoints, including mobile devices and laptops, through anti-malware solutions, and comprehensive security policies.

3. Access Management:

- Implement the principle of least privilege (PoLP), ensuring individuals have access only to the resources necessary for their roles.

4. Incident Response Planning:

- Develop an incident response plan to quickly and effectively address security breaches or attacks when they occur.

5. Secure Software Development:

- If involved in software development, incorporate security measures from the ground up, using secure coding practices and regular code audits.

Maintaining Compliance and Best Practices

1. Understand Legal Obligations:

- Familiarize yourself with legal and regulatory requirements regarding data protection, privacy, and cybersecurity specific to your industry and region (e.g., GDPR, HIPAA).

2. Cybersecurity Frameworks and Standards:

- Adhere to established cybersecurity frameworks and standards, such as NIST or ISO 27001, to guide your security practices and policies.

3. Privacy Policies:

- Ensure transparent privacy policies are in place, informing clients and employees about how their data is collected, used, and protected.

Conclusion

For professionals navigating the digital landscape, cybersecurity is not optional but a crucial aspect of ethical practice, legal compliance, and reputational management. By understanding the risks and implementing robust security measures, professionals can protect themselves, their clients, and their organizations from the potentially devastating impact of cyber threats. Continuous learning, vigilance, and adopting a security-first culture are key to staying ahead in this ever-evolving field.

Chapter 7: Adaptability and Continuous Learning

Adaptability and continuous learning stand as the bedrock principles in the rapidly evolving professional landscape. The capacity to adapt to changing environments and circumstances—and the commitment to perpetual learning—are not just advantageous skills but essential survival tools in today's world. This comprehensive note delves into the importance of these attributes, strategies for cultivation, and their impact on professional growth and innovation.

The Importance of Adaptability and Continuous Learning

1. Navigating Change:

In an era characterized by rapid technological advancements, economic shifts, and global interconnectedness, change is the only constant. Adaptability allows professionals and organizations to navigate these changes, transforming potential challenges into opportunities for growth.

2. Enhancing Employability:

The willingness to continuously learn and adapt ensures that professionals remain relevant and competitive in the job market. It fosters a mindset that is proactive rather than reactive, preparing individuals for future roles that may not yet exist.

3. Fostering Innovation:

Adaptability paired with continuous learning creates a fertile ground for innovation. It encourages experimentation, risk-taking, and the application of new knowledge to solve complex problems.

4. Building Resilience:

These skills imbue individuals and organizations with resilience, enabling them to withstand setbacks and recover more quickly from failures by viewing them as learning opportunities rather than insurmountable obstacles.

Cultivating Adaptability and Continuous Learning

1. Develop a Growth Mindset:

Believe in the potential for growth in intelligence and abilities. View challenges as opportunities to learn rather than tests of innate capacity.

2. Stay Curious:

Cultivate curiosity about your field, adjacent fields, and the world. Ask questions, seek new experiences, and remain open to diverse perspectives.

3. Embrace Failure:

View failure as part of the learning process. Analyze setbacks critically and constructively, extracting lessons and applying them to future endeavors.

4. Seek Feedback:

Regularly seek and constructively use feedback from colleagues, mentors, and networks. Feedback is invaluable for identifying areas for improvement and new directions for learning.

5. Leverage Technology:

Use technology to access learning resources, including online courses, webinars, and peer networks. Technology can provide personalized, flexible learning experiences that fit your pace and interests.

6. Set Learning Goals.

Establish SMART learning objectives, which stand for precise, measurable, achievable, relevant, and time-bound. Regularly review and adjust these goals to maintain direction and motivation.

7. Foster a Culture of Learning:

For organizational leaders, fostering a culture that encourages experimentation, supports risk-taking, and rewards continual learning is crucial for collective adaptability and innovation.

Impact on Professional Growth and Innovation

1. Career Advancement:

Professionals who exhibit adaptability and a commitment to continuous learning are more likely to advance their careers, taking on leadership roles and successfully navigating the complexities of the modern workplace.

2. Organizational Agility:

Organizations that prioritize these skills are better positioned to respond to market changes, adopt new technologies, and remain competitive in their industry.

3. Innovation and Problem Solving:

A workforce that is adaptable and continuously learning is more innovative and effective at problem-solving, contributing to the development of new products, services, and processes that drive growth and success.

4. Employee Engagement and Satisfaction:

Engagement and job satisfaction are higher among professionals who feel they are growing and learning, resulting in lower turnover rates and a more motivated workforce.

Conclusion

In the dynamic and complex environment of the 21st century, adaptability and continuous learning are not optional; they are essential. By embracing these principles, professionals not only ensure their own relevance and success but also contribute to the resilience, innovation, and excellence of their organizations. Cultivating these skills requires intentional effort and a supportive culture, but the rewards—both personal and professional—are profound and enduring.

Embracing Change in the Business Environment

In today's fast-paced and ever-evolving business environment, the ability to embrace change has become a crucial trait for organizations aiming to remain competitive and relevant. Change, whether driven by technological advancements, market shifts, regulatory updates, or consumer behavior, presents both challenges and opportunities. A comprehensive approach to embracing change involves understanding its dynamics, preparing for its inevitability, and strategizing for its successful implementation. Below is a detailed exploration of embracing change in the business environment.

Understanding the Nature of Change

1. Types of Change:

Change in the business environment can manifest in various forms, including technological updates, shifts in consumer preferences, changes in the regulatory landscape, or even global economic trends. Recognizing the type of change your organization is facing is critical to formulating an appropriate response.

2. Speed and Scale of Change:

Change can occur incrementally or in significant leaps. It may have an impact on one department or the whole company. Understanding both the speed and scale of change is essential for appropriately timing and sizing your response.

Preparing for Change

1. Foster a Culture that Embraces Change: Cultivating a corporate culture that views change as an opportunity rather than a threat is foundational. This involves encouraging flexibility, promoting continuous learning, and incentivizing innovation at all levels of the organization.

2. Anticipate Potential Changes:
While not all changes can be predicted, many can be anticipated through strategic foresight. This includes regular industry

analysis, monitoring competitor moves, and staying abreast of technological trends.

3. Build Agile Systems and Processes:
Developing systems and processes that can be quickly adapted is crucial. This might mean adopting more flexible organizational structures, streamlining decision-making processes, or investing in scalable technologies.

Strategies for Embracing Change

1. Communication is Key:
Transparent and continuous communication during times of change helps to align stakeholders, mitigate resistance, and foster an environment of trust and collaboration.

2. Invest in Training and Development:

Equipping your workforce with the necessary skills and knowledge to navigate new technologies, processes, or markets is essential. This may involve formal training programs, workshops, or mentorship initiatives.

3. Engage in Strategic Planning:
Effective change management requires strategic planning that includes setting clear goals, identifying potential risks and obstacles, and developing contingency plans.

4. Leverage Leadership and Change Champions:
Strong leadership is essential for navigating change. Leaders should act as role models in embracing change, while change champions can help facilitate and

motivate their peers throughout the transformation process.

5. Monitor, Evaluate, and Adjust:

Embracing change is an ongoing process. It's important to continuously monitor the outcomes of change initiatives, evaluate their success against predefined objectives, and be ready to make adjustments as necessary.

Challenges in Embracing Change

1. Resistance to Change:

One of the biggest obstacles is resistance from employees, which can stem from fear of the unknown, discomfort with new processes, or satisfaction with the status quo. Addressing these concerns directly and empathetically is crucial.

2. Resource Constraints:

Implementing change often requires significant resources, including time, finance, and human capital. Careful planning and prioritization can help alleviate these constraints.

3. Keeping Pace with Rapid Change:

In some industries, the rate of change can be so rapid that it outpaces an organization's ability to adapt. Remaining flexible and fostering a culture of innovation can help organizations keep pace.

Conclusion

Embracing change in the business environment is an intricate process that requires understanding, preparation, and strategic action. It involves developing a culture that is receptive to change, anticipating forthcoming transformations, and implementing effective strategies to manage change. While challenging, successfully embracing change can lead to innovation, growth, and sustained competitive advantage. Organizations that master the art of change management are well-equipped to navigate the uncertainties of the modern business landscape, turning potential disruptions into opportunities for success.

The Role of Curiosity and Openness in Professional Growth

Curiosity and openness are not just desirable traits in the professional realm; they are powerful catalysts for growth, innovation, and success. The willingness to question, explore, and embrace new ideas and perspectives can lead to a deeper understanding of one's field, enhanced problem-solving abilities, and a more fulfilling career journey. This comprehensive note delves into the profound role that curiosity and openness play in professional growth and development.

The Significance of Curiosity and Openness

1. Learning and Adaptability:

Curiosity compels individuals to seek out new information, experiences, and knowledge. This continuous quest for learning not only broadens one's skill set but also enhances adaptability in a rapidly changing work environment.

2. Problem-solving and Innovation:

Curious individuals are naturally inclined to question the status quo, think creatively, and explore unconventional solutions. This mindset fosters innovation, as novel ideas often emerge from a curious exploration of possibilities.

3. Personal Growth and Fulfillment:

Maintaining an open mind and staying curious about different perspectives, cultures, and ideas can lead to personal growth, expanded horizons, and a more enriching professional journey.

4. Building Relationships and Collaboration:

Openness to diverse viewpoints and a genuine curiosity about others can strengthen relationships, foster collaboration, and enable productive teamwork by valuing different perspectives and promoting inclusivity.

Developing Curiosity and Openness

1. Cultivate a Growth Mindset:

Adopt a growth mindset that views challenges as opportunities for learning and growth rather than fixed limitations. Embrace setbacks as learning experiences that contribute to personal development.

2. Explore Varied Perspectives:

Seek out diverse viewpoints, whether through networking with professionals from different backgrounds, reading materials outside your usual scope, or engaging in cross-disciplinary discussions. Embrace the richness of diverse perspectives.

3. Embrace Continuous Learning:

Commit to lifelong learning by actively seeking out new knowledge, skills, and experiences. Engage in professional development, attend workshops, conferences, or online courses that expand your expertise.

4. Foster Curiosity in Problem-solving:
When faced with challenges or obstacles, approach them with a curious mindset, asking questions, exploring different angles, and experimenting with potential solutions.

5. Encourage Feedback and Reflection:
Invite constructive feedback from peers, mentors, and supervisors to gain new insights and perspectives. Take time for self-reflection to assess your strengths, weaknesses, and areas for growth.

Impact on Professional Growth

1. Enhanced Creativity and Innovation:

Curiosity and openness contribute to a more creative and innovative work environment by encouraging exploration, experimentation, and the pursuit of new ideas.

2. Improved Decision-making:

An open mind and a curious approach to decision-making lead to well-informed choices based on a comprehensive understanding of diverse viewpoints and potential outcomes.

3. Career Advancement Opportunities:

Professionals who exhibit curiosity and openness are often sought after for leadership roles and challenging assignments due to their proactive approach, adaptability, and ability to drive positive change.

4. Personal Satisfaction and Well-being: Curiosity and openness lead to personal fulfillment and a sense of accomplishment, as individuals continuously seek growth opportunities, expand their knowledge, and contribute meaningfully to their work and the world around them.

Conclusion

Curiosity and openness serve as cornerstones for professional growth, success, and fulfillment. By fostering these qualities, individuals not only enhance their own potential but also contribute to a more innovative, collaborative, and adaptive workplace culture. Embrace curiosity as a guiding force in your professional journey, keep an open mind to new possibilities, and cultivate a spirit of exploration that propels you towards continuous learning and growth. In doing so, you'll position yourself for a rewarding and impactful career that transcends boundaries and opens doors to endless opportunities for professional and personal development.

Lifelong Learning Strategies and Resources

Lifelong learning has become a necessity in today's rapidly evolving world, where new technologies, industries, and skills emerge continuously. Embracing a mindset of continual education not only enhances professional growth but also enriches personal development and overall well-being. This comprehensive note explores strategies and resources for engaging in lifelong learning, empowering individuals to stay relevant, adaptable, and fulfilled throughout their lives.

Lifelong Learning Strategies

1. Set Clear Learning Goals:

- Define specific, achievable learning objectives that align with your professional aspirations and personal interests. Setting clear goals provides direction and motivation for continuous learning.

2. Diversify Learning Methods:

- Embrace a variety of learning modalities, including online courses, workshops, seminars, self-study, mentoring, and experiential learning.

Diversifying your learning approach enhances retention and engagement.

3. Prioritize Time Management:

- Set aside time in your weekly or daily schedule for learning activities. Prioritizing learning ensures consistent progress and prevents procrastination.

4. Engage in Reflective Practice:

- Regularly reflect on your learning experiences, noting insights, challenges, and areas for improvement. Reflection enhances comprehension and retention of new knowledge and skills.

5. Seek Feedback and Mentorship:

- Solicit feedback from peers, mentors, or instructors to gain valuable insights and guidance on your learning journey.

Mentorship offers personalized support and opportunities for growth.

6. Apply Newly Acquired Knowledge:

- Translate theoretical learning into practical applications by seeking opportunities to implement new skills or concepts in real-world scenarios. Application solidifies understanding and enhances retention.

7. Embrace Continuous Assessment:

- Engage in self-assessment exercises, quizzes, or evaluations to gauge your progress and identify areas that require further attention. Regular assessment promotes accountability and drives improvement.

Lifelong Learning Resources

1. Online Learning Platforms:

 - Platforms like Coursera, edX, Udemy, and LinkedIn Learning offer a wide range of courses on diverse topics, enabling self-paced, accessible learning from leading institutions and experts.

2. Educational Websites and Blogs:

 - Explore educational websites, blogs, and forums relevant to your interests or industry. Sites like Khan Academy, TED Talks, and Medium offer valuable insights, resources, and inspiration.

3. Local Community Colleges and Libraries:

 - Community colleges and public libraries often provide affordable courses, workshops, and access to educational resources, fostering a sense of community and collaborative learning.

4. **Professional Associations and Workshops**:

- Join professional associations related to your field to access industry-specific events, workshops, and networking opportunities. Engaging with peers enhances learning and career advancement.

5. **Podcasts and Webinars**:

- Podcasts and webinars offer convenient ways to learn on the go. Subscribe to relevant podcasts or attend webinars hosted by thought leaders and experts in your area of interest.

6. **Book Clubs and Discussion Groups**:

- Participate in book clubs or discussion groups focused on learning and personal development. Collaborative learning environments stimulate dialogue, critical thinking, and new perspectives.

7. Social Media and Online Communities:

- Engage with online communities on platforms like Twitter, LinkedIn, or Reddit to follow discussions, share insights, and connect with like-minded learners. Social media is a great place to find information and inspiration.

Lifelong Learning Benefits

Professional Growth and Career Advancement:

Lifelong learning enhances your skill set, boosts employability, and opens doors to new opportunities for career progression and advancement.

Intellectual Stimulation and Personal Development:

Continuous learning fosters intellectual curiosity, creativity, and personal growth, enriching your understanding of the world and broadening your perspectives.

Adaptability and Resilience:

Lifelong learning equips you with the adaptability and resilience needed to navigate changing environments, tackle new challenges, and stay relevant in a dynamic job market.

Enhanced Well-being and Fulfillment:

Engaging in lifelong learning promotes a sense of purpose, accomplishment, and overall well-being, contributing to a fulfilling and meaningful life.

Conclusion

Lifelong learning is a transformative journey that empowers individuals to embrace personal and professional growth throughout their lives. By adopting effective strategies, utilizing diverse resources, and prioritizing continuous education, you can expand your knowledge, skills, and perspectives, ultimately enhancing your career trajectory and enriching your overall quality of life. Embrace the opportunities for learning that surround you, cultivate a thirst for knowledge, and embark on a lifelong learning adventure that propels you towards success, fulfillment, and continuous self-improvement.

Chapter 8: Creating and Maintaining a Professional Image

Creating and maintaining a professional image is essential in the workplace and beyond. A strong professional image not only impacts how others perceive you but also influences your credibility, opportunities for advancement, and overall success. This comprehensive note explores key elements of creating and sustaining a professional image, covering appearance, behavior, communication, and online presence.

Appearance and Image

1. Dress Appropriately:

- Dress according to the expectations of your industry and workplace. Well-fitted, clean, and professional attire conveys competence and respect for the work environment.

2. Personal Grooming:

-Continue to practice proper grooming and personal hygiene.. Attention to grooming details like neat hair, trimmed nails, and clean shoes contributes to a polished professional appearance.

3. Accessories and Details:

- Pay attention to accessories and details that complement your outfit without being distracting. Choose accessories that are tasteful and understated to enhance your overall look.

4. Body Language:

-A firm handshake, eye contact, and proper posture are all important. Positive body language conveys confidence, professionalism, and respect in interpersonal interactions.

Professional Behavior

1. Punctuality and Reliability:

- Arrive on time for meetings, appointments, and deadlines. Demonstrating punctuality and reliability establishes you as a trustworthy and conscientious professional.

2. Work Ethic and Initiative:

- Demonstrate a strong work ethic by taking initiative, meeting deadlines, and going above and beyond in your responsibilities. Look for chances to grow and develop proactively.

3. Professionalism in Communication:

- Use clear, concise, and professional language in all communications. Whether written or verbal, maintain a respectful and courteous tone with colleagues, clients, and superiors.

4. Conflict Resolution Skills:

- Approach conflicts constructively, seeking solutions that benefit all parties involved. Effective conflict resolution fosters positive relationships and demonstrates professionalism under pressure.

Effective Communication

1. Active Listening:

-Engage in active listening by paying close attention to what others are saying when they speak. Show empathy, ask clarifying questions, and provide thoughtful responses to demonstrate respect and understanding.

2. Clear and Concise Messaging:

   - Communicate ideas and information clearly and concisely. Avoid jargon or overly technical language when speaking with non-experts, ensuring your message is easily understood.

3. Professional Email Etiquette:

   - Maintain professional email communication by using proper salutations, clear subject lines, and professional language. Proofread your emails for errors before sending.

4. Public Speaking Skills:

   - Develop strong public speaking skills by practicing speaking in front of groups, organizing your thoughts logically, and engaging your audience effectively. Effective public speaking builds confidence and enhances your professional image.

Online Presence and Branding

1. LinkedIn and Social Media Profiles:

- Update and maintain professional profiles on platforms like LinkedIn. Showcase your skills, achievements, and professional experiences to build a strong online presence.

2. Professional Networking:

- Engage in professional networking events, industry conferences, and online networking groups to expand your connections, exchange ideas, and build a strong professional network.

3. Personal Branding:

-Describe your personal brand and distinctive value proposition. Consistently communicate your strengths, expertise, and professional goals to establish a strong and authentic professional identity.

4. Online Reputation Management:

- Monitor your online presence regularly, ensuring that your public profiles and activities reflect your professional image positively. Be mindful of the content you share and engage with on social media.

Conclusion

Creating and maintaining a professional image is a continuous process that requires attention to detail, self-awareness, and a commitment to excellence. By focusing on appearance, behavior, communication, and online presence, you can cultivate a strong professional image that reflects your credibility, competence, and professionalism. Consistent effort in building and sustaining your professional image will not only enhance your reputation but also open doors to new opportunities, relationships, and career advancement. Embrace the principles of professionalism in every aspect of your professional life, showcasing your best self and contributing to a successful and fulfilling career journey.

- Personal Branding Basics

The deliberate process of creating and marketing a distinct identity that sets you apart from other professionals in your industry is known as personal branding. It involves leveraging your skills, strengths, values, and experiences to cultivate a strong and authentic professional image. This comprehensive note explores the basics of personal branding, covering key elements, strategies, and benefits for building a successful and distinctive personal brand.

Understanding Personal Branding

1. Identity and Differentiation:

- Personal branding is about defining who you are, what you stand for, and how you are distinct from others in your industry. It helps you showcase your unique value proposition and stand out in a competitive market.

2. Consistency and Authenticity:

- The foundation of personal branding lies in consistency and authenticity. Your personal brand should reflect your true self, values, and professional identity across all platforms and interactions.

3. Audience Perception:

- Personal branding is not just about how you see yourself but also about how others perceive you. It involves shaping the narrative around your expertise, achievements, and reputation to create a positive impression.

Key Elements of Personal Branding

1. Purpose and Vision:

- Define your personal brand purpose and vision. Identify your goals, values, and what you want to be known for in your professional sphere.

2. Target Audience:

- Understand your target audience, including colleagues, clients, employers, or industry peers. Make sure the messaging associated with your personal brand speaks to their needs and expectations.

3. Unique Value Proposition (UVP):
- Identify your unique selling points, skills, experiences, and qualities that set you apart from others. Your UVP communicates why people should choose you over competitors.

4. Brand Messaging:
- Craft a compelling brand message that communicates your expertise, values, and achievements succinctly. Throughout all channels of communication, your messaging should remain the same.

Strategies for Building Your Personal Brand

1. Define Your Brand Story:

   - Tell your story authentically, showcasing your journey, experiences, challenges, and successes. A compelling brand story resonates with your audience and creates emotional connections.

2. Create a Consistent Online Presence:

 - Develop a professional online presence through platforms like LinkedIn, personal websites, and social media. Present your expertise, interact with your audience, and share worthwhile content.

3. Network and Build Relationships:

   - Engage in professional networking, attend industry events, and connect with colleagues, mentors, and influencers. Building strong relationships enhances your visibility and credibility in your field.

4. Demonstrate Thought Leadership:

- Establish yourself as an expert in your niche by creating and sharing insightful content, participating in industry discussions, and contributing to relevant publications or platforms.

Benefits of Personal Branding

1. Increased Visibility and Recognition:

- A strong personal brand enhances your visibility within your industry, making you more recognizable and memorable to potential employers, clients, and collaborators.

2. Career Advancement Opportunities:

- Personal branding opens doors to new career opportunities, partnerships, and collaborations. It positions you as a sought-after expert in your field and can lead to professional growth.

3. Enhanced Credibility and Trust:

- By building a credible and consistent personal brand, you instill trust in your audience, showcasing your expertise, reliability, and authenticity in all interactions.

4. **Professional Development and Growth**:

- Personal branding encourages continuous self-improvement, skill development, and visibility in your industry. It contributes to your professional growth and advancement in your career.

Conclusion

Personal branding is a powerful tool for defining your professional identity, communicating your value, and establishing yourself as a trusted authority in your field. By carefully crafting your personal brand and consistently showcasing your skills, expertise, and values, you can differentiate yourself, attract opportunities, and build a reputation that resonates with your target audience. Embrace the fundamentals of personal branding, engage authentically with your audience, and watch as your distinctive personal brand propels you towards success, fulfillment, and professional recognition.

Networking and Professional Associations

Networking plays a crucial role in professional growth and development, and one effective way to network within a specific industry or field is by joining professional associations. Professional associations are organizations formed by individuals with a common profession, interest, or goal to promote and advocate for their field. Here is a comprehensive note on networking and professional associations:

Networking:

Networking is the process of connecting with other professionals, individuals, or organizations to share information, knowledge, resources, and opportunities. It is an important instrument for both personal and professional development.

Effective networking can help you:

1. **Build Connections:** Networking allows you to establish relationships with professionals in your field, potential employers, mentors, and peers. These connections can provide support, guidance, and opportunities throughout your career.

2. **Access Opportunities**: Through networking, you can gain access to job openings, partnerships, collaborations, and professional development opportunities that may not be publicly available.

3. **Exchange Knowledge:** Networking enables you to share ideas, information, best practices, and expertise with others in your industry. This knowledge exchange can enhance your skills and understanding of current trends and practices.

4. **Enhance Visibility:** By networking, you can increase your visibility and credibility within your industry. Building a strong professional network can help you establish a positive reputation and personal brand.

5. **Gain Support:** Networking provides a platform to seek advice, feedback, and

support from experienced professionals and mentors. This support system can be valuable in navigating challenges and making informed career decisions.

Professional Associations:

Professional associations are organizations that bring together individuals in a specific profession or industry to support, promote, and advance their collective interests. These associations offer various benefits to their members, including:

1. **Networking Opportunities**: Professional associations organize events, conferences, seminars, and networking sessions that allow members to connect with peers, experts, and potential employers within their industry.

2. **Professional Development**: Many professional associations offer

workshops, training programs, certifications, and resources to help members enhance their skills, knowledge, and competencies.

3. Advocacy and Representation: Professional associations advocate for the interests, rights, and welfare of their members. They may engage in lobbying, policy development, and industry initiatives to promote the profession.

4. Information and Resources: Members of professional associations gain access to industry publications, research reports, job listings, and other valuable resources to stay informed about current trends, practices, and opportunities.

5. Community and Support: Joining a professional association provides a sense of belonging and a community of like-minded professionals who can offer advice, mentorship, and support throughout your career.

In conclusion, networking and professional associations are essential components of professional success and development. By actively engaging in networking opportunities and becoming a member of relevant professional associations, you can expand your professional connections, enhance your skills, stay updated on industry trends, and advance your career effectively.

- Ethics and Professionalism in Sales and Marketing

Chapter 9: Global Business Etiquette and Cultural Competency

Global business etiquette and cultural competency are crucial aspects of conducting business in an increasingly interconnected world. Understanding and respecting cultural differences, norms, and practices can lead to successful cross-cultural communication, relationships, and partnerships. Here is a comprehensive note on global business etiquette and cultural competency:

Global Business Etiquette:

Global business etiquette refers to the accepted norms, behaviors, and customs that govern professional interactions in a global context. Observing proper business etiquette is essential for building trust, showing respect, and avoiding misunderstandings in international business dealings. Key considerations for global business etiquette include:

1. Respect Cultural Differences: Different cultures have varying expectations regarding communication styles, dress codes, greetings, meeting protocols, and gift-giving. It is important to research and understand the cultural norms of the countries or regions where you conduct business.

2. Communication: Effective cross-cultural communication involves being mindful of language barriers, non-verbal cues, tone of voice, and listening actively. Avoiding jargon, speaking slowly and clearly, and adapting your communication style to accommodate cultural differences can enhance understanding.

3. Professionalism: Demonstrating professionalism in global business interactions involves being punctual, well-prepared, and respectful. Treat your counterparts with courtesy, maintain eye contact, and be mindful of hierarchical structures and titles in different cultures.

4. Gift-Giving: Gift-giving practices vary across cultures, and it is essential to understand the appropriate etiquette for presenting gifts in different countries. In some cultures, gift-giving is a common practice, while in others, it may be seen as inappropriate or bribery.

5. Dining Etiquette: Business meals are a common way to build relationships in many cultures. Understanding dining etiquette, such as table manners, seating arrangements, and customs related to food and beverages, can help you navigate business meals successfully.

Cultural Competency:

Cultural competency refers to the ability to understand, communicate effectively, and work with individuals from diverse cultural backgrounds. Developing cultural competency is essential for building trust, fostering collaboration, and avoiding cultural misunderstandings in global business settings. Key aspects of cultural competence include:

1. **Self-Awareness**: Understanding your own cultural values, biases, and assumptions is the first step toward cultural competency. Reflecting on how your own cultural background influences your perceptions and behaviors can help you develop empathy and openness toward other cultures.

2. **Respect and Empathy**: Cultivating respect, empathy, and curiosity toward

different cultural perspectives is essential for building trust and strong relationships in a global context. Acknowledging and valuing cultural differences can enhance cross-cultural communication and collaboration.

3. **Adaptability:** Being adaptable and flexible in adjusting your behavior, communication style, and practices to align with the cultural norms of your counterparts demonstrates cultural competency. Adapting to different cultural contexts shows respect and openness to diversity.

4. **Continuous Learning**: Cultivating a mindset of lifelong learning and curiosity about different cultures is key to developing cultural competency. Stay informed about global trends, practices, and cultural nuances to navigate cross-cultural interactions effectively.

5. Conflict Resolution: Cultural differences can sometimes lead to misunderstandings or conflicts in business relationships. Developing skills in conflict resolution, active listening, and diplomacy can help you address and resolve cultural differences constructively. In conclusion, global business etiquette and cultural competency are essential skills for navigating the complexities of international business. By understanding and respecting cultural differences, cultivating cultural competency, and practicing proper business etiquette, professionals can enhance cross-cultural communication, build strong relationships, and drive success in global business environments.

Understanding Cultural Differences

Understanding Cultural Differences

Cultural differences refer to the variations in beliefs, behaviors, customs, and norms between different groups of people. These differences can be observed in various aspects such as language, religion, social interactions, communication styles, traditions, and values. Appreciating and understanding cultural differences is crucial in today's globalized world as it helps in fostering respect, empathy, and effective communication among individuals from diverse backgrounds. Here are some key points to consider when understanding cultural differences:

1. **Respect:** Respect for other cultures is fundamental in understanding cultural differences. It involves recognizing that

each culture has its own value system and way of life which should be acknowledged and appreciated.

2. Open-mindedness: Being open-minded allows individuals to approach different cultures without biases or preconceived notions. It enables one to embrace new perspectives and experiences.

3. Communication: Effective cross-cultural communication involves being aware of linguistic differences, non-verbal cues, and cultural nuances that can impact interactions. It's essential to communicate clearly and respectfully.

4. Cultural Sensitivity: Sensitivity to cultural differences involves being mindful of diverse customs, traditions, and practices. It means being aware of potential cultural taboos and avoiding unintentional offense.

5. Empathy: Empathy plays a crucial role in understanding cultural differences. Putting oneself in another person's shoes helps in appreciating their viewpoints and experiences.

6. Cultural Intelligence: Cultural intelligence refers to the ability to function effectively in different cultural contexts. It involves adapting one's behavior and communication style to bridge cultural gaps.

7. Education and Awareness: Educating oneself about various cultures through books, travel, or cultural exchanges can enhance one's understanding of cultural differences. Increased awareness leads to greater tolerance and acceptance.

8. Conflict Resolution: Understanding cultural differences is essential in resolving conflicts that may arise due to misunderstandings or differences in values. It enables individuals to find common ground and work towards mutual understanding.

In conclusion, understanding cultural differences is not only a matter of knowledge but also a mindset that promotes harmony, acceptance, and cooperation in a diverse world. By valuing and respecting the uniqueness of each culture, individuals can build meaningful connections, promote inclusivity, and contribute to a more harmonious global community.

Effective Cross-Cultural Communication

Effective Cross-Cultural Communication
Conceptual exchange between people from different cultural backgrounds is known as cross-cultural communication.

It plays a critical role in today's interconnected world where individuals and organizations are increasingly diverse. Successful cross-cultural communication requires awareness, sensitivity, and adaptation to bridge the communication gap between individuals with varied cultural norms, values, and practices. Here are some essential tips for effective cross-cultural communication:

1. **Cultural Awareness**: Understanding the cultural norms, traditions, and values of others is crucial for effective communication. This awareness helps in interpreting behaviors and messages in the appropriate cultural context.

2. **Respect**: Showing respect for other cultures is essential. Acknowledge and appreciate cultural differences and avoid

making assumptions or judgments based on your own cultural perspective.

3. Active Listening: Listening attentively and actively is key to understanding the perspectives of others. Pay attention to verbal and non-verbal cues to grasp the underlying messages accurately.

4. Clarity and Simplicity: Use clear and simple language to convey your message. Avoid jargon, idioms, or slang that may be difficult for individuals from different cultures to understand.

5. Non-verbal Communication: Be aware of non-verbal cues such as body language, gestures, eye contact, and facial expressions. These can vary significantly across cultures and may impact the interpretation of your message.

6. **Adaptability**: Show flexibility and a willingness to modify your communication style to accommodate the other person's cultural preferences. This may include adjusting your tone, pace, or directness in communication.

7. **Cultural Sensitivity**: Be mindful of cultural taboos, customs, and etiquette. Avoid topics or actions that may be considered offensive or disrespectful in the other person's culture.

8. **Ask Questions**: When in doubt, ask clarifying questions to ensure mutual understanding. Seeking feedback and clarification demonstrates your interest in effective communication.

9. Patience and Empathy: Cultivate patience and empathy when communicating across cultures. Understand that misunderstandings may occur, and be willing to navigate through them with understanding and compassion.

10. Feedback and Reflection: Reflect on your own communication style and seek feedback from others to improve your cross-cultural communication skills. Learn from past interactions to enhance future communication experiences.

By being mindful of cultural differences, actively listening, and adapting your communication style, you can enhance your effectiveness in cross-cultural communication. Embracing diversity and fostering intercultural understanding through communication can lead to meaningful connections, mutual respect, and successful collaborations across cultural boundaries.

- International Business Etiquette: Dos and Don'ts

Navigating the complexities of international business requires not only a strong understanding of business practices but also a keen awareness of cultural norms and etiquette. Different countries have unique customs, traditions, and expectations when it comes to business interactions. Adhering to appropriate etiquette demonstrates respect, professionalism, and cultural sensitivity. Here are some key dos and don'ts to keep in mind when engaging in international business:

Dos:

1. Research the Culture: Before engaging in business with individuals from a different culture, take the time to research and understand their customs, values, and communication styles. This demonstrates your commitment to building respectful and harmonious relationships.

2. Dress Appropriately: Dressing according to the cultural norms of the country you are visiting or interacting with is essential. Pay attention to dress codes and etiquette to make a positive impression.

3. Punctuality: Being on time is important in most cultures, but the expectations may vary. Arrive punctually for meetings and appointments to show respect for your counterparts' time.

4. Greetings and Introductions: Learn how greetings and introductions are traditionally done in the culture you are interacting with. Whether it's a handshake, bow, or other form of greeting, follow the local customs.

5. Business Cards: In many cultures, exchanging business cards is a standard practice. Present and receive business cards with both hands and take the time to examine the card before keeping it.

6. Communication Style: Adjust your communication style to suit the cultural preferences of your counterparts. Be mindful of language choice, tone, and non-verbal cues to ensure clear and effective communication.

7. Respect Hierarchies: Some cultures place a strong emphasis on hierarchy and seniority. Show respect to individuals in positions of authority and address them with appropriate titles and formalities.

Don'ts:

1. Assume Homogeneity: Avoid assuming that all business practices are the same worldwide. Respect and appreciate the diversity of customs and etiquette in different cultures.

2. Use of Language: Refrain from using slang, jargon, or colloquialisms that may not be easily understood by individuals from different cultural backgrounds. Keep your language clear and simple.

3. **Physical Contact:** Be cautious with physical contact as cultural norms around personal space and touch may vary. Always respect personal boundaries and avoid gestures that may be considered inappropriate.

4. **Directness:** In some cultures, direct communication may be perceived as rude or confrontational. Be mindful of your tone and approach, and consider using indirect or diplomatic language when necessary.

5. **Gift-Giving**: While gift-giving is a common practice in many cultures, be aware of the cultural norms regarding gifts. Avoid extravagant or overly personal gifts that may be misconstrued.

6. **Discussions on Sensitive Topics**: Steer clear of sensitive topics such as politics,

religion, or controversial issues unless it is appropriate and relevant to the business discussion. Respect differing viewpoints and maintain professionalism.

By following these dos and don'ts of international business etiquette, you can build strong relationships, foster trust, and navigate the nuances of global business dealings with grace and cultural sensitivity. Adapting to the customs and expectations of your international partners demonstrates your respect for their culture and strengthens your position as a professional and respectful business representative.

Chapter 10: The Future of Professionalism in Business

The Future of Professionalism in Business

As the business landscape continues to evolve rapidly, the concept of professionalism is also undergoing significant changes. In today's dynamic and interconnected world, professionalism extends beyond traditional norms of attire and etiquette to encompass a wider range of skills, behaviors, and values that drive success and sustainability in the business arena. Here are some key considerations shaping the future of professionalism in business:

1. **Adaptability and Resilience**: In an era marked by rapid technological advancements, globalization, and unforeseen disruptions, professionals need to exhibit adaptability and resilience. The ability to pivot, innovate, and thrive in uncertain environments is becoming increasingly essential.

2. **Digital Proficiency**: Proficiency in digital tools and technologies is no longer a luxury but a necessity for professionals in virtually every industry. The future of professionalism in business hinges on the ability to leverage digital platforms for effective communication, collaboration, and problem-solving.

3. **Emotional Intelligence**: Emotional intelligence, including skills such as empathy, self-awareness, and relationship management, is becoming a cornerstone of professionalism. The

capacity to understand and navigate complex human interactions is vital for effective leadership and team dynamics.

4. Diversity and Inclusion: The future of professionalism demands a commitment to diversity and inclusion. Embracing diverse perspectives, fostering inclusivity, and cultivating a culture of equity and respect are imperative for sustainable business success.

5. Ethical Leadership: Ethical leadership is a non-negotiable aspect of professionalism in the future. Upholding integrity, transparency, and ethical standards in decision-making and business practices is crucial for building trust with stakeholders and maintaining long-term credibility.

6. Lifelong Learning: The rapid pace of change requires professionals to embrace lifelong learning and continuous skill development. Remaining curious, adaptive, and open to acquiring new knowledge and competencies is essential for staying relevant in a constantly evolving business landscape.

7. **Sustainability and Corporate Social Responsibility**: The future of professionalism in business is closely intertwined with sustainability and corporate social responsibility. Businesses are increasingly expected to operate ethically, minimize environmental impact, and contribute positively to society.

8. **Collaboration and Teamwork**: Effective collaboration and teamwork skills are integral to professionalism in the future. The ability to work harmoniously with diverse teams, communicate clearly, and leverage collective strengths will be key to

driving innovation and achieving shared goals.

9. **Personal Branding**: Establishing a strong personal brand that aligns with one's values, expertise, and professional reputation is becoming crucial in the future of business professionalism. Building a distinct and authentic professional identity can help professionals stand out in a competitive landscape.

10. **Global Competence**: With globalization blurring geographical boundaries, global competence is becoming an essential skill for professionals. Understanding cross-cultural nuances, working effectively in diverse teams, and navigating international business environments are vital for future success.

In conclusion, the future of professionalism in business is characterized by a shift towards a more holistic and adaptive approach that values not only technical expertise but also emotional intelligence, ethical leadership, diversity, and lifelong learning. Embracing these evolving dimensions of professionalism can position individuals and organizations to thrive in an increasingly complex and interconnected business world.

- Trends Influencing Business Professionalism

Business professionalism is continually evolving in response to a variety of trends shaping the modern business landscape. These trends influence how professionals interact, communicate, and conduct themselves in the workplace. To adapt and prosper in the fast-paced business world of today, people and organizations must have a thorough understanding of these trends. Here are some key trends influencing business professionalism:

1. **Remote Work**: The rise of remote work has transformed traditional notions of professionalism. Professionals are now navigating virtual workspaces, requiring a high level of self-discipline, effective communication skills, and the ability to maintain professionalism in digital interactions.

2. **Flexible Work Arrangements**: Increasingly, businesses are embracing flexible work arrangements such as telecommuting, flextime, and compressed workweeks. This trend demands professionals to demonstrate adaptability

and accountability while balancing work commitments with personal responsibilities.

3. Digital Transformation: The digital transformation of businesses has revolutionized how professionals collaborate, communicate, and deliver services. Proficiency in digital tools and platforms is crucial for maintaining professionalism in a tech-driven workplace.

4. Emphasis on Employee Well-being: Organizations are placing greater emphasis on employee well-being, mental health, and work-life balance. Demonstrating professionalism includes prioritizing self-care, setting boundaries, and advocating for holistic wellness in the workplace.

5. Diversity and Inclusion Initiatives: Businesses are increasingly focusing on diversity and inclusion initiatives to create more equitable and inclusive work environments. Professionals are expected to uphold values of respect, empathy, and inclusivity in their interactions with colleagues from diverse backgrounds.

6. **Sustainability and Corporate Social Responsibility**: The growing emphasis on sustainability and corporate social responsibility is influencing business professionalism. Ethical considerations, environmental stewardship, and social impact are integral aspects of demonstrating professionalism in a socially conscious world.

7. **Gig Economy and Freelancing**: The rise of the gig economy and freelance work is reshaping traditional employment models. Professionals engaging in freelance or contract work must exhibit professionalism through reliability,

quality of work, and effective communication with clients and collaborators.

8. AI and Automation: The integration of artificial intelligence and automation in business processes is redefining professional roles and skill requirements. Professionals need to adapt to working alongside AI, upskill in tech-related competencies, and demonstrate agility in embracing AI-driven tools.

9. **Personal Branding and Thought Leadership**: Professionals are leveraging personal branding and thought leadership to stand out in a competitive marketplace. Establishing a strong professional presence online, sharing expertise through content creation, and engaging with industry trends are essential for maintaining relevance and credibility.

10. **Globalization and Cross-Cultural Communication**: Globalization has expanded business boundaries, necessitating proficiency in cross-cultural communication and global competence. Professionals must navigate cultural nuances, adapt to diverse working styles, and demonstrate cultural sensitivity to succeed in international business settings. These trends underscore the evolving nature of professionalism in the business world and highlight the importance of adaptability, digital fluency, ethical practices, and inclusivity in defining what it means to be a professional in today's dynamic and interconnected business landscape. Staying attuned to these trends and proactively embracing change can help individuals and organizations thrive in an ever-evolving professional environment.

- The Impact of Artificial Intelligence and Technology

Artificial intelligence and technology have fundamentally transformed nearly every aspect of society, including business, healthcare, education, communication, and more. The rapid advancement and integration of AI and technology are reshaping how individuals work, interact, and live. The impact of AI and technology is profound and multifaceted, influencing various aspects of daily life and the future trajectory of society. Here are some key areas where artificial intelligence and technology are making a significant impact:

1. **Automation and Efficiency**: AI-driven automation is streamlining processes, increasing efficiency, and reducing manual labor across industries. Tasks that were once time-consuming and repetitive can now be automated, allowing professionals to focus on higher-value work.

2. **Enhanced Decision-Making:** AI technologies enable data-driven decision-making by analyzing vast amounts of information to derive insights, identify patterns, and predict outcomes. Businesses can make more informed decisions based on accurate data analysis and forecasting.

3. **Personalization and Customer Experience:** Technology is enabling personalized experiences for consumers through targeted marketing, customized

recommendations, and tailored services. AI algorithms analyze user preferences and behavior to deliver personalized content and services.

4. Healthcare Innovation: In healthcare, AI is revolutionizing diagnostics, treatment planning, and patient care. Medical professionals can leverage AI-powered tools for medical imaging analysis, predictive analytics, personalized medicine, and telemedicine, leading to improved patient outcomes.

5. Workforce Transformation: The integration of AI and technology is transforming the nature of work and the skills required in the workforce. Professionals need to adapt to technological advancements, upskill in digital competencies, and collaborate effectively with AI systems and robots.

6. Environmental Sustainability: Technology plays a crucial role in promoting environmental sustainability through tools for monitoring, conservation, and renewable energy. AI algorithms can optimize energy consumption, reduce waste, and enhance environmental efforts across industries.

7. Cybersecurity and Privacy: With the increasing digitalization of data and transactions, cybersecurity and privacy have become paramount concerns. AI is used to detect and prevent cyber threats, enhance data encryption, and secure sensitive information from cyber-attacks.

8. Education and Learning: Technology is revolutionizing education through online learning platforms, adaptive learning systems, virtual classrooms, and interactive educational tools. AI-powered education platforms personalize learning experiences, provide real-time feedback, and support remote learning initiatives.

9. Transportation and Mobility: AI and technology are driving innovations in transportation and mobility, including autonomous vehicles, ride-sharing platforms, traffic management systems, and smart infrastructure. These advancements aim to improve safety, efficiency, and sustainability in transportation networks.

10. Ethical and Social Implications: The widespread adoption of AI and technology raises ethical considerations around data privacy, algorithm bias, job displacement, and societal impact. It is essential to address these ethical and social implications to ensure responsible and equitable use of technology.

In conclusion, the impact of artificial intelligence and technology is far-reaching, transforming industries, societies, and individual lives in profound ways. Embracing the potential of AI and technology while addressing ethical concerns and ensuring responsible use is essential for harnessing the benefits of technological advancements and shaping a future that is sustainable, inclusive, and innovative. By understanding and adapting to the impact of AI and technology, individuals and organizations can leverage technological advancements to drive progress and create positive change in a rapidly evolving world.

- Preparing for the Future of Work

The future of work is rapidly evolving, driven by technological advancements, changing demographics, and global economic shifts. To thrive in the increasingly dynamic and competitive landscape, individuals and organizations must anticipate and prepare for the transformations ahead. Preparing for the future of work entails developing a combination of technical skills, soft skills, and adaptability to navigate the challenges and opportunities that lie ahead. Here are some key strategies for individuals and organizations to prepare for the future of work:

1. **Lifelong Learning**: Embrace a mindset of continuous learning and skill development. Stay abreast of industry trends, emerging technologies, and best practices to remain relevant and competitive in the evolving job market.

2. **Digital Literacy**: Enhance your digital literacy by acquiring proficiency in digital

tools, software applications, and online platforms. Develop skills in data analysis, cloud computing, cybersecurity, and other tech-related competencies that are increasingly in demand.

3. Soft Skills Development: Cultivate essential soft skills such as communication, collaboration, critical thinking, problem-solving, emotional intelligence, and adaptability. These skills are highly valued in the workplace and are essential for effective teamwork and leadership.

4. Adaptability and Resilience: Build resilience and adaptability to thrive in fast-changing work environments. Embrace ambiguity, learn to pivot in response to challenges, and maintain a positive attitude in the face of uncertainty.

5. Remote Work Skills: Develop remote work skills for effective virtual collaboration, time management, communication, and productivity. Adapt to the hybrid work model by mastering digital communication tools and establishing routines that support remote work success.

6. Industry Networking: Build a strong professional network within your industry by attending conferences, seminars, and networking events. Connect with peers, mentors, and industry experts to gain insights, exchange ideas, and explore new opportunities.

7. Entrepreneurial Mindset: Foster an entrepreneurial mindset by seeking out innovative solutions, taking calculated risks, and seizing opportunities for growth and development. Think creatively, proactively, and strategically in approaching challenges and projects.

8. Diversity and Inclusion Awareness: Enhance your awareness of diversity and inclusion practices in the workplace. Foster an inclusive mindset, celebrate diversity, and promote equity and respect for all individuals in the work environment.

9. Embrace Change: Embrace change as a constant in the future of work. Be open to new ideas, feedback, and ways of working. Agility and adaptability will be critical skills in navigating evolving industry trends and organizational needs.

10. Professional Branding: Develop a strong professional brand by showcasing your expertise, accomplishments, and unique value proposition. Create an online presence through social media, professional networks, and personal branding initiatives to enhance your visibility and credibility in your field.

By proactively preparing for the future of work through continuous learning, skill development, adaptability, and a growth mindset, individuals can position themselves for success in a rapidly changing work environment. Embracing the opportunities and challenges of the future of work with resilience, creativity, and a commitment to lifelong learning will empower individuals to thrive in a dynamic and competitive professional landscape.

Conclusion of the book Business Professionalism

Business professionalism is a cornerstone of success in the modern workplace, essential for building credibility, fostering positive relationships, and achieving professional excellence. Throughout our exploration of the topic, it becomes evident that professionalism extends beyond mere adherence to dress codes or etiquettes; it encompasses a deeper set of values, behaviors, and skills that define an individual's conduct and reputation in a business setting.

By understanding and practicing concepts such as cultural awareness, effective communication, ethical behavior, and adaptability, professionals can navigate the complexities of today's diverse and rapidly changing work environments. The ability to communicate respectfully across cultures, demonstrate empathy and emotional intelligence, and maintain a strong ethical compass are key attributes of a truly professional individual.

The future of business professionalism is likely to be shaped by ongoing trends such as digital transformation, remote work, sustainability, and diversity and inclusion. Professionals who embrace lifelong learning, develop digital proficiency, champion ethical leadership, and prioritize well-being and inclusivity will be well-positioned to succeed in the evolving landscape of work.

In conclusion, business professionalism goes beyond surface-level appearances; it is about embodying integrity, respect, and excellence in all interactions and endeavors. By upholding the principles of professionalism and adapting to the changing demands of the business world, individuals can establish themselves as trusted, respected professionals who contribute positively to their organizations and broader society.